BUSHPLANES

Geza Szurovy

ZENITH PRESS

First published in 2004 by Zenith Press, an imprint of MBI Publishing Company, Galtier Plaza, Suite 200, 380 Jackson Street, St. Paul, MN 55101-3885 USA

ISBN 0-7603-1478-0

Acquisitions Editor: Dennis Pernu
Editor: Amy Glaser
Design by LeAnn Kuhlman

Printed in Malaysia

On the cover: A deHavilland DCH-2 Beaver comes in for a water landing. *Geza Szurovy*

On the frontispiece: This Alaska Southern Airways advertisement is still a popular feature in the waiting rooms of modern bush operators.

On the title page: An Otter is the star attraction in a timeless scene on an Alaskan waterway.

On the back cover, top right: Properly refurbished Beavers can fly forever. *Top right:* Max Ward observed that the Otter's ability to carry 4x8-foot plywood sheets, a mainstay of construction, profoundly changed lives by bringing affordable, easy-to-construct mainstream housing to the small, scattered settlements deep in the wilderness. This Alaskan Otter still carries wooden sheets for constructing remote lodges. *Bottom right:* The Republic SeaBee was a postwar personal amphibian that many bush operators used for light duties. The verdict was mixed. Everyone agreed it was underpowered with its 215-horsepower Franklin engine, but some found its large cabin appealing and it was widely used in summer operations.

Photo credits: Alaska Aviation Heritage Museum: 10, 20, 24, 26 top, 35, 36, 39 bottom, 40, 42-46, 50-52, 57, 58 right, 90, 93, 100, 102, 104, 108, 112, 158 top left, *Alaska Department of Tourism:* 149 *Anchorage Museum of History:* 22, 32, 34, 49, 74, 77, 80, 83, 105, 110, 118 bottom, 128, 130 right, *Antique Airplane Association:* 69, *Bombardier:* 128, *Canadian Bushplane Heritage Center:* 8, 11, 12, 14-19, 26 bottom, 28, 30, 31, 38, 39 top, 58 left, 59-63, 66-68, 71, 73, 78 top, 79, 85, 87, 92, 94, 113, 117, 118 top, 121, 123, 124 left, 126, 127, courtesy *Jim Dodson:* 54, 55, 130 left, Royal Australian Flying Doctor Service: 64, courtesy *Jim Ruotsala:* 97, 140, *Seattle Museum of Flight, Gordon Williams Collection:* 154, *United States Air Force:* 76, 81, 84, 88, 89, *Richard Vander Meulen:* 37

All other photography by author or from author's or other private collections.

Contents

Acknowledgments

This book would not have been possible without the assistance of many dedicated custodians of bushflying's history, and the cooperation of operators, pilots, and ground staff of numerous bushflying services.

I owe a great debt of gratitude to the Canadian Bushpilot Heritage Center in Sault Ste. Marie, Ontario; home of the trailblazing Ontario Provincial Air Service and its successor organizations. I would like to particularly thank archivist Terry White and museum staff, Harvey Hobbs, and Jack Minor. CBHC's excellent photo archives provided an opportunity to present many unique photographs of bushflying's early days for the first time in print.

Thanks also go to Air Dale for a most pleasant time on Ranger Lake and an insight into the workings of a modern day bushflying service, and to Richard and Linda Smith of Eastbourne Manor for their hospitality.

I would especially like to thank Jim Dodson of Anchorage, who selflessly shared his family's pioneering bushflying history and memorabilia. Jim grew up in the family business, Jim Dodson Air Services, which was run by his parents out of Ruby and Fairbanks, and provided a rare direct link to those early days.

Thanks also to the Alaska Aviation Heritage Museum on the Lake Hood seaplane base in Anchorage, and its executive director, Dee Hanson, who allowed the use of photographic resources at a time when the museum was in a challenging state of transition.

Thanks to Kathleen Hertel, curator of the Anchorage Museum of History for assistance with photographs, many of which are published here for the first time.

Among Alaska's bush flying services, thanks to Todd and Suzanne Rust of Rust's Flying Service for allowing me generous access to their operations based at Lake Hood and at Talkeetna, the airstrip that serves Mt. McKinley and the Denali National Park region.

Thanks are especially due to Wings of Alaska of Juneau and its chief pilot, Mike Stedman, who personally showed me the aerial haunts of Shell Simmons, Frank Barr, and others; and thanks to his uncle Bill of Petersburg, whose memoirs of a lifetime spent flying the panhandle, mostly in a Grumman Goose, were invaluable. Thanks also to Bob Bedford, who started his career maintaining the aircraft of Alaska Coastal Airlines in the early days and finished up on the jets of Alaska Airlines; and to Jim Ruotsella for sharing his vast knowledge of Alaskan aviation history.

I am also grateful to Dennis Pernu and Amy Glaser, my editors at MBI Publishing, for making this book possible.

Introduction

It was still light when the jetliner from the East Coast landed at Anchorage International Airport at 10:00 p.m. on a summer night. The first impression of Alaska its disembarking passengers had was the drone of a radial engine overhead. They glanced up to see a bushplane outlined against the fading light as it took off from the nearby Lake Hood seaplane base on its last flight for the day.

The sight of a radial-engined, high-wing floatplane over Alaska and the world's other wilderness areas has remained unchanged for nearly 75 years. In our modern world, the best way to reach many wilderness destinations where the only airport is one provided by nature, remains an airplane that has more in common with the airplanes that pioneered bush flying in the 1920s and 1930s than it has with modern aircraft. Flying bushplanes remains the last opportunity to experience aviation as it was in its early days. Modern navigation aids, such as GPS, have found their way into the bushplane's cockpit and have brought greater safety and utility, but bushpilots still fly mostly by the seat of their pants. They rely mainly on their own judgment to beat the weather and land and take off on lakes, sandbars, glaciers, and open tundra as generations of bushpilots have done before them.

Bushplanes provides an overview of bushflying with a primary focus on Canada and Alaska. It highlights developments and events that were key to establishing reliable air service in the wilderness. It presents many rare, never before published photographs from important museum collections in North America to illustrate the story. While it is beyond the book's scope to provide an all encompassing history of bush flying worldwide, sidebars provide a sampler of bushflying in other parts of the world, including Australia and Africa.

Chapter 1

A two-man crew and an Ontario forestry official prepare for a forest survey flight in a Curtiss HS-2L flying boat. Their mission will accomplish in a few hours what it would take the official weeks to do by canoe and on foot.

By the Seat of Their Pants

O n a blustery late November morning in 1931, on frozen Wolf Lake in Canada's Yukon Territory, bush pilot Frank Barr's heart sank as he emerged from the fur trapper's cabin where he had spent the night. His tiny Cirrus Puss Moth, which he had flown in the night before from Atlin, British Columbia, about 120 air miles to the south, lay flat on its back with its skis pointing defiantly skyward. It had been flipped and crumpled by the storm that raged overnight, despite Barr's best efforts to tie it down securely. The Moth's wing fabric was torn in several places, a number of wing ribs were broken, and the leading edge of one wing was crushed. A structural wing strut holding the upper and lower wings together had buckled, and about 6 inches were missing from one tip of the two-bladed wooden propeller.

The stocky, soft-spoken pilot's options were disheartening. He was on his way to deliver cans of gasoline to a remote mining exploration site for the spring prospecting season but was now grounded with no way to inform anyone of his predicament. He had only the most basic set of emergency tools with him and knew there was no airplane in the region that could be expected to search for him. His only companions were a couple of native fur trappers who would soon leave for weeks to check their lines.

Barr could try to slog 60 miles on snowshoes across a mountain range to Teslin, the nearest settlement. At a time of year when the nightly temperatures dipped as low as 50 degrees below 0, it was a risky, unappealing proposition that had earlier claimed the life of another pilot in a similar predicament. Barr chose an alternative possibility, one that would seem even more

Frank Barr is pictured with his Fairchild American Pilgrim. The Pilgrim was an airliner that quickly became obsolete, but was valued by bush pilots for its large cargo capacity and excellent short and rough field performance.

hopeless to anyone but a bush pilot, given the Moth's condition in the frozen, empty wilderness. He would try to repair the airplane and fly it out.

Barr's decision was motivated by his sense of self-preservation and by commercial considerations, a perpetual concern for early bush pilots whose shoestring operations forever courted financial disaster. If he abandoned the Moth, he wouldn't be able to return and fix it until the spring or early summer, and by the time he was done, he and his employer would have missed almost a whole season of work and income.

Barr and the trappers removed the Moth's wings, flipped the fuselage upright, and he set to work. A paste of boiled moose fat served as rudimentary glue for the damaged fabric. He nailed scavenged wood bits to the cracked wing ribs to restore their stiffness. He bridged the damaged area of the wing strut with the wooden handle of an axe that he tied in place as tightly as he could with moose-hide twine. He fixed the crumpled leading edge by covering it with panels fabricated from one of the gasoline cans he was transporting for the mining company. He used his hunting knife and a paper template to carve off the good propeller tip to match the tip that was missing 6 inches.

To sustain himself during the repairs, he dipped into the prodigious stocks of dried food he carried for such an occasion. He also caught rabbits with snares borrowed from the trappers and shot ptarmigan with his .22-caliber rifle.

It took him six weeks in total solitude, working with his bare hands for seconds at a time before slipping on his bulky gloves to warm his fingers for another brief round of repairs. On Christmas

An Ontario Provincial Air Service HS-2L flying boat is in its element. These aircraft were first operated by Laurentide in the wilderness in 1919 and are generally acknowledged as the first to be used in a bush flying role.

Day he put on his snowshoes and trampled out a half-mile-long runway on frozen Lake Wolf. The next morning he fired up the plumber's torch he carried to warm the engine and its oil, squeezed himself into the Cirrus Moth, and started the engine on the first try. He eyed the length of the makeshift runway and opened the throttle.

At the moment of truth, the Moth lazily took to the air. Like so many bush pilots before and after him, Frank Barr found out that his crude field repairs, which would prompt any government airworthiness inspector to ground him on the spot, had degraded, but not destroyed, his airplane's performance. With every wobbly mile behind him, he felt more confident that he would make it. For most of the flight, he warily eyed the axe handle that held together the damaged wing strut. He also sneaked occasional glances at the endless forest below where he knew he wouldn't find a single emergency field if the makeshift strut failed him.

In an hour he reached Teslin, where he refueled and spent the night. The next day, after another uneventful hour aloft, he touched down at Atlin, his point of departure six weeks before.

In following decades Frank Barr flew hundreds of thousands of tons of freight across northern Canada and Alaska. He amassed thousands of flight hours, most of them routine and some laced with more adventures that challenged his innermost resources. In the end he won every challenge bush flying had to throw at him. He died at age 79 in 1983.

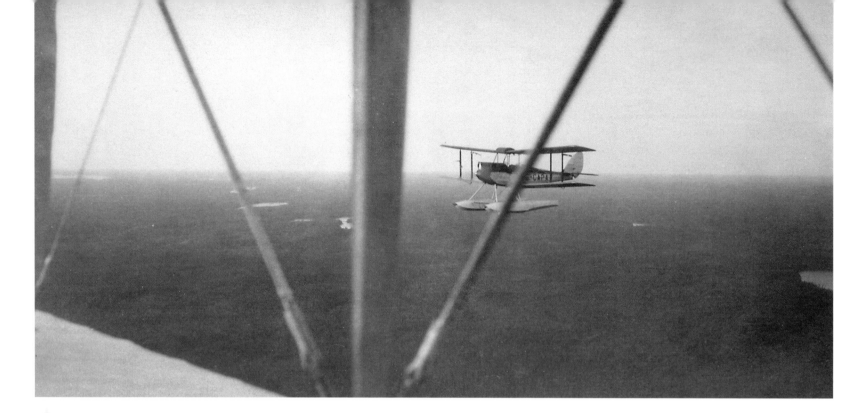

A Puss Moth similar to the one Frank Barr flew is seen through the flying wires of an HS-2L. It was said that if a canary flew in between the maze of flying wires, it would never find its way out.

Defining Bush Flying

Barr's Wolf Lake escapade conveys the concept of bush flying, a term that is loosely defined and used on several levels to describe flying under harsh conditions. For many people, flying off dirt strips with little reliance on radio navigational aids fit their definition of bush flying. Purists retort that true bush flying involves off-airport takeoffs and landings—on sandbars, fields, exposed mountain ridges, or bodies of water. There isn't a single answer to what bush flying is, but the consensus lies somewhere between the extremes and has evolved over the years.

It could be argued that in the beginning, all flying was bush flying. Airplanes took off from dirt strips or bodies of water, their pilots found their way by the seat of their pants, and they landed on dirt strips, lakes, and rivers, relying only on their own resources. This was what it was like in the early days of the barnstormers but only for a short time. The airport and airway infrastructure that connected large population centers developed rapidly throughout the world as aviation became commercialized and offered pilots increasing guidance and ground support.

By the late 1920s, pilots in most populated areas could depart from well-equipped airports with every mechanical need of their aircraft met prior to departure. Armed with weather briefings, they could find their way along marked airways to their destination. Their biggest challenge was bad weather, but if the flight got too tough, the prudent pilot could land at any number of emergency fields dotting the route. If the destination was a simple landing field with little or no service, a more sophisticated airport was never far away.

By the mid-1930s, airliners along the busier airways routinely rode radio beams and with the help of their instruments landed with sufficient certainty, maintaining schedules with more than 80 percent reliability. In spite of the popular perception that aviation was dangerous, air passenger insurance was bought at almost the same rate as rail passenger insurance.

Meanwhile Down Under

From an early aviator's point of view, Australia could be thought of as an oversized Alaska or Canada's Northwest Territories without the winter. Australia is an area almost the size of the continental United States, and in 1919, it was populated by only 5 million people spread out along the coast and throughout its vast interior desert, known as the Outback. Ninety percent of the country was accessible only on horseback or foot. The trains that ran along some coastal sections could take three to four days between principal cities. Instead of the forbidding Alaskan winters, there were searing Australian summers when the temperature in the shade could stay at 130 degrees Fahrenheit for weeks. During the wet season, massive thunderstorms unleashed flooding of biblical proportions.

Aviation was brought into this environment by Australian airmen who returned from World War I. To publicize the promise of the airplane, a London-to-Sydney air race was organized in 1919. Of the seven participants only two made it to Australia, but the symbol of their extraordinary achievement was enough. There were heroes' welcomes galore, and from then on Australia was one of the world's most air-minded nations.

One of its first bush services was formed by two ex-Royal Flying Corps pilots, Hudson Fysh and P. J. McGinness. They were hired to scout suitable emergency landing fields in the north for the participants of the 1919 air race. As they conducted their search over the desolate scrubland, they quickly recognized the potential to provide air service to the widely scattered ranches. Backed by profitable ranchers, they launched their air service in 1921 with two war surplus British biplanes and called it Queensland and Northern Territory Aerial Service, QANTAS for short. Today it is one of the most global and oldest continuously operating airlines in the world.

The British Avro 504 World War I surplus trainer was the first QANTAS aircraft.

Another pioneering bush service was Norman Brearley's Western Australian Airways, located in Perth, more than 2,000 miles across the continent from Queensland. It began operations with war surplus aircraft. Both air services received air mail contracts that helped them weather the typical financial uncertainties of the early bush-flying years and become major airlines. Other bush services quickly sprang up and brought an ordinary, normal life to people in places where there was no other good way to go, just like in the Alaskan and Canadian wilderness. Bush flying also served other important needs as Australia's mining industry prospered and the Flying Doctor Service was formed. Bushplanes continue to be an indispensable part of everyday life down under.

Commercial aviation became increasingly safer, sophisticated, and reliable. Yet there was an area of flying that posed the same challenges as the earliest days, when pilots could expect little support from the ground, and more often than not, success depended on the ingenuity and resourcefulness of the pilot and the mechanic who occasionally rode along.

This was the world of flying in wilderness areas, or "the bush." Here, settlements were sparse or absent, ground transportation was nonexistent or painfully slow and often seasonal, and there was no

"Alaska keeps you guessing."

—Noel Wien

A forestry crew arrives in the bush by a flight of flying boats. In a dramatic demonstration of the aircraft's potential in 1921, a flying boat spotted the beginnings of a forest fire and landed a single ranger who put it out. Thousands of acres would have burnt before the fire was even noticed had it not been for the aircraft.

infrastructural support for aviation. Three factors caught the attention of adventurous aviators looking for new opportunities in these areas. Remote settlements, many of which could be completely cut off from the world for months at a time, craved more frequent contact with the outside. The biggest challenge for individuals and companies specializing in the discovery, extraction, and management of natural resources was accessing their areas of operation. In those days, a diminishing but vibrant community of explorers was keen to unravel the final geographic mysteries of a planet that still offered areas to be discovered and explored.

If the airplane could reliably operate in such environments, it would be the perfect vehicle for the wilderness. Airplanes could transport people, equipment, and provisions in hours, rather than the weeks or months it takes by ground. Airplanes would make wilderness travel more convenient and raise activity and productivity in the bush to a level that was hitherto unimaginable. The airplane and bush flying played a revolutionary role in opening the wilderness to human use.

The airplane's potential for increasing access to remote areas was first recognized in the aftermath of World War I. Companies began to establish operating bases at permanent settlements in the deepest reaches of the bush. From there, people could venture into the boundless, often hostile, and barely known lands that lay beyond.

The first bush pilots are generally acknowledged to have been Canadian aviators. As pilots and mechanics returned by the thousands from World War I, the aircraft that had served in the war were

sold at bargain prices on the civilian market. Schemes to use the planes for a profit abounded. One of the more imaginative ideas came from the Laurentide Company, a major Canadian paper mill headquartered in Montreal, Quebec.

Laurentide owned thousands of acres of forest in the province, and one of its big problems was identifying and controlling forest fires. Another challenge was accurately mapping its holdings to better manage them. Laurentide realized the perfect vehicle for vastly expanding its capabilities in both functions was the airplane. Landplanes were a problem in the vast tracts of forest, but the thousands of lakes and rivers made the territory ideal for the flying boat, a specialized form of aircraft that had come into its own flying coastal patrols during the war.

Laurentide's choice of flying boat was the Curtiss HS-2L. Several were sold to Canada by the U.S. Navy, and two were loaned to the company by the Canadian government. The large 3 1/2-ton biplane was a good choice by the standards of the day in spite of its unwieldy handling characteristics, unreliable Liberty engine, and anemic takeoff performance. It had more than 300 miles of range, could carry a hefty load, and its rugged hull was well suited for withstanding the stresses of taking off and landing on water.

Aerial mapping was one of the first uses of aircraft in the wilderness. An aircraft could accomplish in a few months what it would take land surveyors years to do.

The first "H boats," as the Canadians called them, started operations in the summer of 1919 from their base on Quebec's Lac a la Tortue, 645 miles north of Montreal. Over the next three seasons, in between the winter freezes, they markedly improved Laurentide's fire-detection and mapping capabilities at a cost the company eventually looked to offset. For the 1922 season, the company spun off the flying boat operation into a new arm's-length venture called Laurentide Air Services, run by W. Roy Maxwell, a flamboyant former RAF pilot. Outside investors were invited to participate in the new venture.

With the additional investments, the company acquired so much potential business, including contracts extending deep into Ontario to the west, that it bought 14 surplus HS-2Ls to handle its new commitments. In addition to their effectiveness at spotting forest fires, the flying boats also dramatically demonstrated how aviation's ability to increase productivity would fundamentally change the manner in which large-scale surveying had been done for centuries. Requested to map a large tract of forest in Ontario, a pair of H boats accomplished as much work in one month of aerial photo mapping as land surveyors did in six years.

Most of the work that Laurentide performed in Ontario was for the provincial government, whose Forestry Service managed most of the province's immense timber resources. Ontario's government had good reason to seek a revolutionary new way to improve its control over forest fires. In the five years that preceded its experiments with airplanes, the organization had relied on 1,200

Here is an early bush pilot in his office. A number of pilots who started out in open cockpit bushplanes in the 1920s and 1930s ended their careers in command of intercontinental jet airliners.

This is a forestry official's hand-drawn map of Canadian timber resources. Sketched in flight, it identifies tree types, age, forest density, and other technical details.

rangers paddling 600 canoes to patrol the forests. Ontario was losing almost 1 million acres of timber annually to forest fires. The great Haileybury fire of 1922 was a huge disaster that torched 1.3 million acres of forest, claimed 44 lives, and caused $6 million of damage.

By the time the rangers out on foot patrols or in their canoes discovered the fires, most were out of control. A dramatic example of the airplanes' effectiveness was exhibited for the first time in 1921 when the crew of an H boat on an experimental map-sketching mission spotted the beginnings of a fire near a lakeshore. The crew promptly flew in a single ranger who put out the fire before it got out of control. Without the H boat's services, thousands of acres could have been lost.

Ontario's provincial government was so impressed by Laurentide's performance that it entered the business of aerial patrolling and surveying because it would be less expensive than hiring seasonal contractors. In 1924 it formed the Ontario Provincial Air Service (OPAS) and lured Roy Maxwell away from Laurentide to run it, first putting the pioneering bush-flying firm out of business and then buying its fleet of 13 H boats. Located on the shore of Lake Huron in Sault Ste. Marie, OPAS became one of the world's largest, most skilled, and most enduring bush-flying operations. Its successor organization is still going strong, 80 years later, and its first hangar is now the Canadian Bush Flying Museum.

The Ontario Provincial Air Service's home base in Sault Ste. Marie is shown in this photograph from the 1920s. OPAS operated over a dozen HS-2L flying boats.

North to Alaska

As the early successes of Laurentide and OPAS inspired the rapid growth of bush flying throughout Canada, bush flying took its first tentative steps in Alaska, that other great North American wilderness. It became one of the most natural habitats of the bushplane.

Alaskans were introduced to the airplane as early as 1913, when the town worthies of Fairbanks invited James Martin and his wife, Lilly, who was also a pilot, to bring their Gage-Martin biplane up from Seattle and demonstrate it over Fairbanks' baseball park on July 4. Promoters planned to sell tickets to the event to pay for the stiff expenses of bringing the couple and their flying machine to Fairbanks. James Martin, an East Coast consulting engineer and early airplane builder, accepted the invitation and shipped his airplane to Fairbanks via one of the toughest routes of the Alaska Gold Rush in 1898.

The first stage was by steamer to Skagway, north of Juneau in southeastern Alaska. The airplane was then put on the famous White Pass and Yukon narrow-gauge railway (which tourists can still ride from Skagway to Whitehorse in the Yukon Territory) and transported 800 miles by riverboat down the Yukon River and another 100 miles up two tributaries to Fairbanks. It was certainly a tremendous effort for a one-day flight demonstration, but was well worth it for those who had never seen the miracle of flight—and the town was paying the freight.

Martin made four short flights and the town was suitably enthralled. But the promoters lost their shirts because everyone could see all the aerial action without having to pay to enter the ballpark.

A Canadian flying boat crew takes a lunch break between flights at Sturgeon Lake near Thunder Bay in 1926. Crews spent weeks at a time at lakeshore forward bases, which were not much more than a depot for fuel and basic supplies.

Here is a pair of Canadian Vickers Vedette flying boats. Smaller than the H boats, they were used for aerial mapping.

Although they were unwieldy and underpowered, the H boats are remembered with pride for the bush flying foundations they laid over 75 years ago. The map is a modern day fire patrol's mission map and records their flight's details in grease pencil in Ontario's Red Lake area.

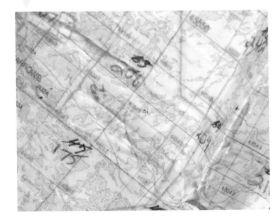

It was seven years before airplanes were seen over Alaska again. In 1920 the Army Air Corps came out in force on a marathon flight from New York City to Nome, Alaska, with four de Havilland DH-4s (the same airplanes used by the early air mail service) to demonstrate the revolutionary reach of air power. Their expedition went off without a hitch and many in the large Alaskan crowds they drew wondered when aviation would gain a permanent toehold in their territory.

The bona fide start of Alaskan bush flying can be pinpointed to two years later when Roy Jones, an ex-Army flier in search of an opportunity to continue flying, decided to set up Alaska's first commercial air service. Before he became a pilot, Jones hauled gasoline and other petroleum products in boats to canneries in southeastern Alaska. He correctly saw this maze of islands and isolated coastal towns, cut off from the rest of the world by water and the nearly impenetrable Coast Mountains, as one of the most suitable environments for an air service.

Given the island environment where every settlement was on the water, Jones' choice of aircraft was, like Laurentide's, a flying boat, an ex-Navy Curtiss MF Seagull biplane powered by a 180-horsepower Hispano-Suiza engine. He christened it *Northbird* and called his business Northbird Aviation Company. Supported by a personal mechanic, Jones flew joyriders, mining officials, salesmen, government agents, supplies, and fish throughout Alaska's southeast. His ports of call included Ketchikan, Wrangell, Juneau, Skagway, and many other settlements that to this day are routine stops on the bush pilot's beat. Jones was also a frequent caller at the region's many salmon canneries that were then in their heyday, most of them previously accessible only by slow boat.

The first year was a success for the Northbird Aviation Company and Jones enthusiastically commenced the 1923 season. Midway through the summer, on a flight to Heckman Lake north of Ketchikan to drop off a client who managed a fish hatchery there, his luck ran out. On departure, the *Northbird* was forced back onto the small lake by downdrafts. It hit hard, its hull was punctured, and the plane sank. Jones and a passenger along for the ride scrambled out of the wreck with minor scratches, but the airplane couldn't be salvaged. With his proverbial financial shoestring in tatters, Jones lacked the resources to remain in business and headed south. Six years passed before commercial aviation returned to Alaska's southeast.

As Jones wound up the affairs of the Northbird Aviation Company, Alaskan aviation got its first sustained toehold up north in Fairbanks, the town that residents called Alaska's "Golden Heart." The man of the hour was Ben Eileson, whom many Alaskans regard as their first bush pilot.

Eileson was a lanky, enthusiastic North Dakotan of Scandinavian descent who went to Alaska to teach school in 1922. He had qualified as an Army pilot during World War I, but his family vehemently opposed his plans to continue flying after the war. He reluctantly resumed his law studies in Washington, D.C., but found the experience stifling and bolted to Alaska to teach math and science. He enjoyed his new life in Fairbanks but hankered for the sky. In 1923, he found a way back into the cockpit.

With the help of "Wrong Font" Thompson, the editor of the *News-Miner*, Fairbanks' most influential newspaper, and a committed aviation booster, Eileson convinced a group of local businessmen to fund an air service in the interest of the community. While Alaska's interior has its share of water surfaces, the opportunities to operate off dry land are greater and, consequently, so were the choices of aircraft for pioneer aviators. Eileson's group set modest goals and settled on a war surplus Curtiss Jenny with an OX-5 engine, the aircraft in which Eileson had most of his flying experience.

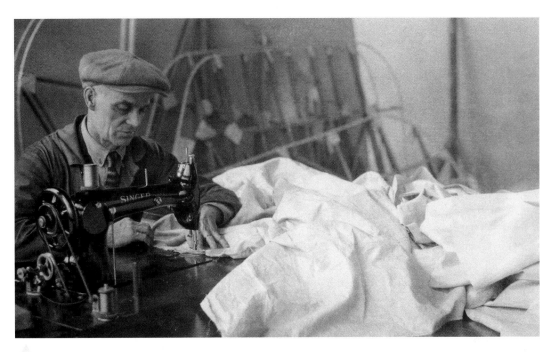

Fabric repair skills were important to keep the bush planes airworthy in the 1920s. Fabric tears were common even in the most minor incidents, and a major crash inevitably required recovering at least some part of the airframe.

Engine change, bushplane style. The cranky liquid-cooled Liberty engine of this H boat has failed and is being replaced. Bush mechanics and pilots worked under trying conditions and learned to improvise. Note the engine stand made of logs.

19

FLYING MACHINE TAKEN AT FAIRBANKS ALASKA - ALASKA SHOP-

Ben Eielson and Noel Wien, Alaska's first bush pilots, flew rudimentary surplus World War I training airplanes, such as this Curtiss Jenny seen in Fairbanks shortly after being shipped to Alaska.

Ben Eielson arrives from Fairbanks at McGrath with the U.S. Mail in 1923, challenging the postal dog teams. The experimental service was discontinued because Eielson kept crashing at the inadequate fields. But the airplane could cover in an hour the distance a dog team took a week to mush.

The Jenny was shipped to Fairbanks and assembled just in time to make its first flight on July 4, 10 years to the day after James Martin's flight demonstration from the same ballpark. For the inaugural flight Eileson carried Fairbanks banker Dick Wood, one of his principal backers. Their destination was Nenana, 50 miles west along one of the few railroad tracks in the territory.

In spite of the short hop, Eileson decided to take a shortcut away from the railroad line, which turned out to be a mistake. He became disoriented over the featureless terrain and circled frantically for an hour and a half before he figured out where he was and limped into Nenana. But the town's residents, unfamiliar with estimated flight times, gave the pair a hero's welcome anyway, and the next day Eileson dazzled them with aerobatics at which he was apparently quite skilled.

Eileson settled down for the rest of the summer and shuttled passengers and what little cargo the fragile Jenny could accommodate between Fairbanks and nearby settlements. His exploits were eagerly followed by the community, which developed a close affinity for "their" air service, a trait that became a common sentiment toward local air services throughout Alaska's settlements in the following years. By summer's end, Thompson contentedly editorialized in his newspaper that Eileson "has demonstrated what aerial traffic could do for this country."

Eileson's next break came early the following year when he managed to convince the U.S. Post Office to award him Alaska's first air mail contract and ship him a de Havilland DH-4 mail plane to go with it. The experiment called for 10 air mail flights during the year between Fairbanks and the town of McGrath, 280 miles away and otherwise connected only by dogsled trail, like so many of the territory's settlements. Eileson received $2 per mile from the post office, less than half the rate paid to the dogsled teams. In return, he was expected to deliver the mail in a little more than three hours compared to the 20 days it took the dogsled teams. It promised to be the end of an era and the dawn of an epochal step forward in the name of technical progress, revered in those days with an almost religious conviction. But in reality the dogs were to be reprieved for a few more years. The air mail experiment proved to be more demanding than darting out to nearby communities in the Jenny, and it was plagued by the difficulties posed by Alaska's forbidding environment.

For the first flight, in the dead of winter on February 21, 1923, Eileson had a set of wooden skis custom-made for the DH-4 by a Fairbanks carpenter. It was one of the first experiments with a form of landing gear that soon became standard for bush flying on snow and ice. Eileson's flight to McGrath went without a hitch, but by the time he could break away from the celebrations of the inaugural flight perilously little light remained in the short Alaskan winter day and he didn't arrive back in Fairbanks until dark. Bonfires guided him to the ballpark, but he flipped the airplane on its back upon landing at the short field.

Two more of the next seven flights also ended in crashes and the post office asked for its airplane back after the last one, which prematurely ended Alaska's first experiment with air mail and put Eileson's bush-flying career on hold. Undaunted, the pioneering bush pilot headed for Washington to promote Arctic flying and procure additional air mail contracts. He lost a bid against the dog teams for the 1925 contracts and didn't return to Alaska until the following year.

The early bush pilots who approached the vast unknown mountain ranges had no idea what they were getting into and couldn't afford any mistakes exploring them.

Noel Wien (left) and a passenger are pictured besides one of the Standards he flew for Jimmy Rodebaugh's Fairbanks Aviation Company in 1925. The Standards had a brisk business flying enthusiastic prospectors, government officials, and others into wilderness destinations, saving them weeks of travel time. Flying supplies to bush dwellers was an equally important business.

Noel Wien, in a Fokker III, is about to depart on the first flight between Fairbanks and Nome, a distance of 540 miles, in June 1925. The only land alternative was the 750-mile dogsled trail. The mayor of Nome is handing Wien a piece of commemorative mail.

Generating Goodwill

Eileson may have suffered a personal setback with a skeptical post office, but he generated tremendous goodwill for aviation in Fairbanks and throughout Alaska. A steady trickle of fliers appeared and laid the foundations of bush flying in the territory and made the airplane as indispensable to Alaskans as the automobile is to outsiders.

The first among this new breed of aviator was Noel Wien, who became one of Alaska's most successful and highly respected aviation entrepreneurs. Over a lengthy career, Wien nurtured his various companies into an airline, flying a fleet of the most modern Boeing jetliners. But when the former Minnesota farm boy and barnstormer got off the boat from Seattle at Seward, Alaska, in 1924 and headed to Anchorage, he found a job flying Standard J-1s, open-cockpit war surplus biplanes almost identical to the Curtiss Jenny. Wien's employer was Jimmy Rodebaugh, a senior conductor on the Alaska Railroad who moonlighted as an aviation entrepreneur. Rodebaugh scraped together $5,000 to buy two of the Standards, making his Fairbanks Aviation Company the largest air service in Alaska.

One of Wien's first jobs was to reposition one of the Standards from Anchorage to its permanent base in Fairbanks. The 350-mile flight was the first between the two cities and, more impressively, the first across the formidable Alaska Range, crowned by 20,320-foot Mt. McKinley. Leaving at 2:30 a.m., first light on that long Alaska summer day, Wien and his mechanic, Bill Yunker, largely followed the route of the Alaska Railroad. They passed over Talkeetna (which later became the base for McKinley's mountain fliers) and skirted Mt. McKinley to the east as they struggled up to 8,000 feet and cleared the lowest pass on the Alaska Range.

Noel Wien's Stinson Detroiter (foreground) and Russ Merrill's Travel Air were forced down above the Arctic Circle in 1928 when they were flying a Fox film crew to Point Barrow, America's northernmost settlement. Wien got out, but Merrill was stuck because of the Travel Air's small tires and set off one of Alaska's first epic rescue expeditions of stranded air travelers.

Wien had trouble following the railroad, which constantly disappeared into mountain tunnels, and he was amazed by the utter lack of any place to land across the range. They made it safely across only to be confronted on the last leg to Fairbanks by an immense cloud of smoke that stretched across the horizon—a forest fire that slashed visibility to less than a quarter-mile. Without sufficient gas to turn back, Wien let down quickly as close to the ground as he dared and glued the Standard to the railroad tracks. Yunker acted as lookout while Wien concentrated on the tracks, and they groped their way to Fairbanks and landed safely.

Following this tense arrival, Wien settled down to bread-and-butter flying, the first Alaskan pilot to regularly provide the kind of services that have become standard bush pilot fare. Mines extracting gold, silver, copper, zinc, lead, and other minerals were important clients, as were prospectors, fur traders, and salesmen. Flying bales of fur and pokes of gold dust worth thousands of dollars out of the bush was as routine as flying in supplies and transporting passengers. The clientele, adventurous Alaskans, flocked to flight and relished the ability to get done in a day what could take as much as three weeks by ground.

The Standards provided an express lifeline to the outlying communities and brought them essential items such as fresh meat and medicines that couldn't wait for the dog teams. They flew in the occasional doctor or dentist and took their inhabitants into town on matters of urgency or just for a welcome break. They also began performing what quickly became the bushplane's most highly valued service in Alaska: the medical emergency flight.

Wien had no reliable maps to show the way, and none of his destinations had a proper airstrip. He flew by following rivers, streams, and dog trails and memorized every little landmark that was helpful, learning to orient himself by reference to hills and mountains, and gingerly landing on the most welcoming patch of flat ground. Gravel bars, hard packed and even, proved to be some of

Russ Merrill's Travel Air CW cabin biplane on Lake Spenard in Anchorage is about to take off on a supply run. The pilot is still out in the breeze, but there is an enclosed four-person cabin under the bales of cargo.

the most reliable landing spots. Sandbars were softer but also consistent. Frozen rivers and lakes were good options at the right time of year and only after careful visual inspection for smoothness on a low pass or two.

Wien's logbook provides useful insight into these early flights. His first assignment was to fly a wealthy Fairbanks banker to a tiny sandbar at Livengood, 50 air miles to the northwest, to inspect his gold claims, a trip that would have taken at least four days over land. It was the first of about 30 flights that year to Livengood, a community of around 250 miners.

On another occasion Wien took a Bureau of Mines inspector to Eagle on the U.S.–Canadian border. Over land, the inspector used to take three weeks to make the trip. Going by airplane he was back in Fairbanks by midafternoon on the same day. One trip to another mine took Wien several days due to bad weather, but his passengers were still delighted and saved two weeks in travel time compared to their traditional alternative. Wien nosed over on landings several times, but with a spare propeller always strapped to its fuselage, the Standard was soon back in the air.

Wien's last trip of his first season was another milestone for Alaskan aviation. It was the first time in the world an airplane crossed the Arctic Circle. Wien was heading for the gold fields at Wiseman with two miners, 185 miles north of Fairbanks and 80 miles beyond the Arctic Circle. But as they crossed the Arctic Circle, they ran into such heavy snow that they had to turn back, ending up at their point of departure after flying more than five hours. Early in the following season Wien reached Wiseman, but on the return trip vicious headwinds and an oil pressure failure forced him down halfway back on the muddy thawing mess of spring tundra, making him the first Alaskan pilot to be marooned in the wilderness. It took him four days to walk out and he lost 20 pounds, but he proved that even in Alaska's harsh environment, down is not always out.

The Fairbanks Airplane Company quickly outgrew the Standards and the following year it acquired a Fokker III, Dutch airplane designer Anthony Fokker's big single-engine, high-wing

Ed Young, Alaska's third bush pilot, clad in the typical pre-Goretex cold weather gear, is pictured next to an appropriately named Pacific Alaska Airlines' Fairchild. Young perished in an air crash near Livengood in the 1930s.

This is a bush pilot's flying jacket from the 1920s at the Canadian Bushplane Heritage Center in Sault Ste. Marie, Ontario.

monoplane. It was unwieldy and ate up a lot of runway, but it could haul five passengers or more than a half ton of cargo, far more than the flimsy Standards.

In this airplane, Noel Wien made the first flight to Nome, the isolated settlement where the Yukon River spills into the Bering Sea. Today this is the northern terminus of the grueling Iditarod dogsled race. When the waters froze during the winter, Nome was reachable only by a 750-mile dogsled trek. Wien's flight didn't go quite as planned because the Yukon River was so high that all the sandbars he was counting on en route to serve as landing spots for refueling were submerged. He had to make an emergency landing on a short field at Nulato, an old ex-Russian trading post. The field was soggy and the heavy Fokker's wheels dug in and it nosed over on its back. Remarkably, only the propeller and the tip of the rudder were casualties. Turning the Fokker right side up was a bigger production than the repairs, but with the whole village of Nulato straining on command, it was eventually accomplished and Wien arrived in Nome only three days late to an ecstatic reception.

A rare restored Travel Air cabin biplane on floats is on Lake Hood in Anchorage, which was connected to Lake Spenard in the 1960s, and is still the world's busiest seaplane base.

Rod Ross, Brent Balchen, Al Cheesman, and Frederick Stevenson in Hudson, Ontario, on April 22, 1927, on their return from airlifting dredges to Hudson Bay in their Fokker Universals. They had flown 12,000 miles on their assignment. Stevenson walked 20 miles out of the wilderness on this trip when his oil pipe burst and he had to make a forced landing.

It was a prophetic trip. In early 1927, after a falling-out with the Fairbanks Airplane Company over its hiring of a questionable pilot, Noel Wien, his brother Ralph, who had traveled north to be a mechanic, and Gene Miller, one of Alaska's first nature photographers and a friend of theirs, joined forces to buy one of the old Standards and launch Wien Alaska Airways, Nome's first air service.

Setting up shop in Nome was one of the Wiens' biggest contributions to early Alaskan aviation. The small village was an important supply and communications hub for scores of tiny outlying settlements and mines on the Seward Peninsula and the Arctic coast that were connected only by dogsled or boat. Wien Alaska Airways brought this region out of decades of isolation. When the company acquired a Stinson Detroiter, one of the first airplanes with an enclosed cockpit, it commenced regular service to Fairbanks. For the first time in its history Nome wasn't cut off from the United States between October and June when the boats stopped sailing for the winter.

The mid-1920s also saw the beginnings of air services in Anchorage, Alaska. Its main protagonists were a group of Anchorage businessmen, including the local Caterpillar and Ford dealer. They hired Alonzo Cope, a jovial railroad mechanic, to organize the venture. Cope approached a thin, easygoing ex-Navy pilot, Russell Merrill, to become the venture's pilot.

Merrill had already been seriously bitten by the Alaskan aviation bug. In 1925 he and a friend, Roy Davis, brought a Curtiss F Model flying boat up the length of the Alaska coast and intended to operate it from the Seward Peninsula, but a hard landing had destroyed the craft. Merrill wrote to friends that he'd rather fly in Alaska and live on beans than fly down in the Pacific Northwest and own a Rolls-Royce, and he jumped at the opportunity offered by Cope.

Cope selected the first two aircraft for the new company. Both were Travelairs made in Wichita, Kansas. They were biplanes: one a four-seat, open-cockpit model, the other a larger aircraft with an enclosed cabin for five ahead of the pilot's open cockpit. Christened *Anchorage 2* and *Anchorage 1*, respectively, they were sent to Alaska in a crate by boat and assembled in early 1927. Ed Young, the third pilot to fly regularly in Alaska, joined the company as second pilot and the Alaska Air Transport Company was ready for business.

Their first few months of operations were plagued with frustrating accidents typical of operating in the bush. On its first test hop *Anchorage 2* caught a ski and ground-looped, breaking its propeller and damaging a wing spar. *Anchorage 1* set off for the Kuskokwim River region with Ed Young, but its cowling was too tightly set to protect the engine from the cold and three cylinders melted, forcing Young down near Bethel. No sooner was *Anchorage 2* repaired that Merrill set off for Lake Iliamna with a fur trader and caught a ski on a buried ice chunk, ground-looping and sustaining further wing damage.

Repaired once again, *Anchorage 2* flew to Nome with Merrill and Cope on a volunteer medical mercy mission to evacuate a patient who died on a nearby island while they were waiting for the weather to improve. Picking up a chance fur-buying charter to Candle before planning to head home to Anchorage, Merrill was trapped by a blizzard and in the emergency landing, the Travelair flipped on its back on Selawik Lake and was severely damaged. Fortunately *Anchorage 1* was back in the air and flew to meet the dog teams towing the wreck of *Anchorage 2* into Candle and took the crew home to Anchorage.

The intrepid aviators put *Anchorage 1* on pontoons (one of the first uses of pontoons in Alaska) to service the salmon canneries around Bristol Bay, about 300 miles west of Anchorage. They based

The Fokker Universals were popular bushplanes, especially in Canada, because of their large cargo capacity for the 1920s and their thick, high lift wings. This one is at Fort Churchill on Hudson Bay.

Millions of acres of northern Canada remain unchanged since the time of Punch Dickins' historic exploration flights. He would not have far to fly from the country's more densely populated southern belt to feel right back in the 1920s.

the airplane on Lake Spenard, today a part of the Lake Hood complex, the world's biggest seaplane base and adjacent to Anchorage International Airport. Shortly after they started the cannery runs a 70-mile-per-hour gale blew over *Anchorage 1* and absolutely totaled it during an overnight stay on Bristol Bay. The reconstruction of the tangled mess over the next few months was nothing short of a resurrection, plagued by the challenge of getting sufficient parts and materials to the cannery by surface transportation. Such tenacity in the face of repeated adversity characterized the attitude of the early bush pilots and it ultimately paid off for Merrill and Cope. For the rest of the year Alaska Air Transport operated without major incident and built its much-needed client base.

Late in the year, Merrill made a lasting contribution to Alaskan aviation when he discovered a new, considerably shorter route from Anchorage through the forbidding Alaska Range to the lucrative fur-trapping regions of the Kuskokwim River. It was a narrow, winding route with a floor of 3,000 feet surrounded by peaks reaching as high as 12,000 feet. It soon was officially known as Merrill Pass and is still a regular route of bush pilots today.

Bush Flying in Canada

While Alaska's budding air services slowly gained experience and took their lumps, Canadian bush flying developed from the early H boat days on a slightly different track. Various national and provincial government organizations and big companies working in wilderness areas were staunch supporters of air transportation and often bought one or an entire fleet of aircraft, operating the planes through a dedicated flight department. But there was also plenty of scope for entrepreneurial adventure.

Canadian bush flying's next burst of activity following the H boat period came from one of the country's biggest gold discoveries in 1925, on Red Lake in western Ontario. It was a tailor-made opportunity for air support. The nearest railhead of the Canadian National Railway came to within 120 miles of Red Lake to Sioux Lookout on Minnitaki Lake. All the supplies the gold fields needed could be stockpiled at the railhead where it was easy to fly them into Red Lake.

This opportunity launched the career of one of Canada's first entrepreneurial bush pilots, Harold "Doc" Oaks. Uncharacteristically, Doc was a geologist and an aviator. He originally came to Red Lake to prospect for gold and stake his claims, but decided he'd sell them and form an air service on the proceeds to serve the miners. He established Patricia Airways and first flew a leased H boat and then a small Curtiss Lark biplane on a single float with enough room for two passengers or 400 pounds of freight and equipment. He remained a one-man operation and hauled all comers and cargoes for the next two years and made as many as a dozen trips during long summer days. In the winter, he switched from the Lark's pontoon to skis, which were coming into use on aircraft.

Oaks quickly became a respected pilot and moved westward with his earnings from the Red Lake gold rush. Together with a Winnipeg grain merchant, he founded his next venture, Western Canada Airways, based in Hudson, Ontario. Besides Oaks, the grandly named one-plane air service employed only mechanic Al Cheeseman and a clerk and hauled freight and passengers to neighboring mines.

Western Canada Airways' big break came when the Canadian government, mindful of Oaks' solid reputation, approached him to perform a major air freight project. The government wanted to build a railroad from Manitoba to Hudson Bay to carry wheat for export to Europe, but the northern ports weren't deep enough for the grain ships. Dredging required massive drilling equipment and the government proposed that Western Canada Airways fly the machinery to Fort Churchill on Hudson Bay from a railhead 125 miles to the south. Oaks accepted and, with his Winnipeg backer, invested in three large, rugged single-engine Fokker Universal monoplanes. He hired Brent Balchen, a Norwegian Arctic flier, and Rod Ross and Frederick Stevenson, two experienced pilots from OPAS.

The group commenced the airlift in late March, racing against the thaw, which would end flying off lakes on skis but would not allow flying on floats until all the ice completely melted much later. In less than a month they hauled 8 tons of equipment and 14 workers to Fort Churchill, completing one of the biggest airlifts performed to date. Some of the individual pieces weighed more than 600 pounds and required crates 20 feet long.

Most of the flights went smoothly, but there were occasional moments of excitement, including a forced landing by Stevenson when an oil line burst. When Stevenson staggered into base camp after an arduous three-day trek across the frozen tundra, he was shocked to see his airplane parked on the ice. His colleagues spotted the abandoned Universal from the air and landed to investigate. They had the tools to fix the broken pipe, and not finding any sign of Stevenson, flew his plane home.

Back to Nome

While Doc and his friends were making their reputation and impressing their government in the Canadian bush, business was so good for the Wiens up in Nome, Alaska, that they added a Hamilton Metalplane to their flight line. The Hamilton was a scaled-down, single-engine predecessor of the Ford Trimotor, which Stout had also designed. Its chief advantages were its easy-to-maintain metal airframe and large cargo capacity, and in it, Noel Wien flew one of the more interesting bush flights of his career.

In early 1929 the Wiens were contacted by the Swenson Herskovits Trading Company of New York, which had an exclusive contract with the Soviet authorities for trading in Siberian fur outside

Noel Wien's Hamilton Metalplane in Nome, Alaska, is where the pilot opened his own air service in 1927. Wien flew this aircraft to retrieve furs from the *Elisif,* which was frozen in the Siberian ice 600 miles from Nome.

the Soviet Union. The Danish fur ship *Elisif* was stuck in the ice with $600,000 worth of the company's white fox pelts off North Cape in Siberia, 600 air miles across the Bering Sea from Nome. The Soviet authorities were receptive to authorize a request for an air rescue of the furs.

Noel Wien weighed the odds. Lack of information about the weather except at Nome and Cape North, which the *Elisif* could radio to Nome, was one challenge. Having almost no hope of rescue if he was forced down on the ice along most of the route was another. There were shorelines to follow for all but about 20 minutes of the actual crossing of the Bering Strait, but he didn't know how well defined the distinction would be between the sea ice and shore ice on the 400-mile Siberian coastal leg. In the end, he concluded it wasn't that much different from the kind of flying he was already doing, and in the spacious Hamilton, he had the ideal airplane for the mission. He accepted and on March 7 set course for Cape North, accompanied by auto repairman Calvin Cripe, who was promoted to aviation mechanic for the trip. In the cabin behind them they packed a whole hog and a quarter of beef for the *Elisif*'s meat-starved crew.

The flight went smoothly by bush pilot standards. The shores were relatively easy to follow, and the weather held. The Hamilton's oil pressure rose alarmingly in the middle of the crossing and threatened to burst the oil tanks as they flew from March 7 into March 8 across the International Date Line, but Wien knew exactly what the problem was. The oil vent on the wing was freezing up. Cripe opened the window in the 60-below temperature (lowered even further by the slipstream's windchill effect) and poked away at the frost with a knife. He repeated the procedure every 15 minutes for the rest of the trip and all was well. The *Elisif* appeared as advertised. A rough landing on the washboard-like ice drifts that were as hard as concrete was aggravated by frozen shock absorbers, but the Hamilton bore it without a scratch. For the first time, an airplane had connected the American continent with Asia.

About one-quarter of the 6,400 fox pelts were crammed into the Hamilton, the tanks were topped off with gasoline provided by the Russians, and Wien set course for home. The engine ran rough the entire way because the Russian gas that had been stockpiled for 10 years had deteriorated. Cripe continued to hang out his window every 15 minutes to scrape frost from the wing's oil vent, and Nome appeared before them in about six and a half hours. Another routine day in the life of the bush pilot.

Wien was prepared to fly three more trips to haul out the rest of the pelts, but the Soviets arbitrarily withdrew permission for the remaining flights.

Some time after the fur flight it became apparent just how established the foundations of aviation had become in Alaska when Aviation Corporation of America (Avco) wanted to buy a string of Alaskan air services. Founded and promoted by the Wall Street investment firms of W. A. Harriman and Lehman Brothers, Avco was a major aviation holding company and snapped up airlines and aircraft manufacturers throughout the United States, including the companies that became American Airlines.

By 1929 Avco had good reason to be interested in the world of bush flying. Aviation's foothold in Alaska had been firmly planted. The territory's 50,000 inhabitants were served by 57 graded landing fields, and territorial and community funds were allocated to support the fledgling aviation infrastructure. Weeks Field, the old ballpark at Fairbanks, acquired a U.S. weather bureau; air hubs had been established at Anchorage, Fairbanks, and Nome; and permanent air service was about to commence in southeast Alaska. There were only 24 aircraft in the territory and barely more pilots, but they flew 340,000 miles during the year, carried more than 17,000 pounds of mail, and hauled more than 100,000 pounds of freight.

A rare candid moment of peace and quiet in the 1920s for an air-minded Canadian couple next to a Fokker Super Universal.

Avco was represented by Ben Eileson, who returned to Alaska two years before to fly for Australian explorer Captain George Wilkins on a quest to open an Arctic air route to Europe. The pair had spent 500 flight hours together probing the Arctic and 13 days on the polar ice cap when engine failure forced them down 300 miles out to sea from Point Barrow. (With incredible luck they eventually stumbled on a fur-trapping post.) In 1928 they made a historic first flight between Alaska and Europe, winging their way nonstop from Point Barrow to Spitsbergen, Norway, in 13 hours in a Lockheed Vega, a type of airplane that later featured prominently in the bush.

Eileson was ready to get back to running an air service and Avco was ready to back him. He selected Wien Alaska Airways, Anchorage Air Transport, and Bennett-Rodebaugh, the successor firm to the Fairbanks Aviation Company. The companies' cash-strapped owners found the big Wall Street firm's offer irresistible. (Wien decided to cash in and go on his honeymoon, four years overdue.) The firms were combined into Alaskan Airways (no relation to today's Alaska Airlines), the first entity with a presence throughout Alaska, except for the southeast where it actively sought an opportunity.

Bush flying had put down tenacious roots in Canada also. Centered on services funded by the governments and major corporations working in the extractive industries, but also having its share of individualistic, entrepreneurial, small-scale operators, aviation became indispensable to the fabric of everyday life in the Canadian wilderness.

Another reason for the imminent upswing in bush flying was the advance in aviation technology, particularly the appearance of more reliable and lighter engines with significantly improved power-to-weight ratios.

Some lamented the end of bush flying's pioneering days, but as air services were set to mushroom in the wildest corners of the planet a series of tragedies claimed the lives of some of the most experienced aviators and provided somber reminders that bush flying was anything but routine.

Chapter 2

Jones and Crosson are pictured with the Stearman and the Fairchild behind it on Muldrow Glacier. This was the same Stearman Gillam flew on the search to find Ben Eielson and Earl Borland over the Bering Sea. Today it is on display at the Alaska Aviation Heritage Museum on Lake Hood in Anchorage. Note the American Airways livery on the airplanes. Alaska Airways was an American Airways subsidiary at the time and was later bought by Pan American.

Shrinking The Bush

On September 16, 1929, Russ Merrill flew back-to-back morning charters from Anchorage's Spenard Lake, the bread-and-butter business of bush operations that are still flying from there today. After taking a hunting guide and supplies to a lake on the Kenai Peninsula, a short flight to the south, he headed northwest for Rainy Pass to drop off another guide at a camp for big-game hunters. Hunting and fishing, which play a critical role in sustaining the demand for bush flying today, were already important businesses for pilots like Merrill.

His job for the afternoon was more traditional. He set off for a mine beyond the Alaska Range near Bethel, where the Kuskokwim River closes in on the Bering Sea. It was a rescue mission of sorts. The mine was shut down while awaiting a replacement compressor securely lodged inside the cabin of Merrill's airplane, *Anchorage 1*. Merrill took off late in the afternoon and intended to spend the night near Steelmute on the Kuskokwim, about halfway to his destination. He was never seen again.

His disappearance set off a massive search led by his Alaska Airways boss Ben Eileson. Other pilots and observers came from throughout Alaska to help in the search. Among them was Joe Crosson, who, despite being only 26 years old, was one of Alaska's most experienced pilots.

Crosson had come to Alaska to fly for the Fairbanks Airplane Company in 1924. He then flew as a support pilot for Captain Wilkins' Arctic and Antarctic expeditions with Ben Eileson and had a summer stint with Western Canada Airways.

When Merrill disappeared, Crosson was returning to Alaska to become chief pilot of the newly formed Alaska Airways. He had just lost his sister, Marvel, who was also a pilot. She crashed in Arizona while participating in the first Women's Air Derby alongside such well-known pilots as Amelia Earhart, Louise Thaden, and Pancho Barnes. Joe and Marvel had learned to fly in California in a Curtiss Jenny they bought together.

Over the next five weeks more than 1,000 hours of flight time were spent in the search for Merrill, much of it by Crosson, but to no avail. On the sixth week a suspicious patch of aircraft fabric turned up along the far shore of the Cook Inlet only 50 air miles from Anchorage. It was the same color as Merrill's plane, and Merrill's partner, Alonzo Cope, recognized his handiwork on the stitching. Russell Merrill's body was never found.

In early October, as the search for Merrill was going on, news came of Ralph Wien's death in a crash at Kotzebue. Wien died trying to land on Kotzebue's tight 750-foot dirt strip in a diesel-powered six-seat Bellanca he was flying for a Jesuit mission. Two of the mission's priests perished with him. Wien came to Alaska to be his brother Noel's mechanic and became an accomplished pilot himself. He wasn't widely known outside the territory, but the local community was hit hard by his death.

The tragedy that happened the following month made headlines worldwide. Ben Eileson and his mechanic, Earl Borland, disappeared on a flight to retrieve pelts from a fur ship stuck in the Siberian ice. The *Nanuk,* sister ship of the *Elisif,* was trapped off North Cape in the same region where Noel Wien had flown to retrieve furs from the *Elisif* the year before (see Chapter 1). Eileson was flying the same Hamilton that Wien had used, which came with Wien's business when it became part of Alaska Airways. This time the financial stakes were higher. Alaska Airways was to receive $50,000 for rescuing the pelts, a major payday for the recently formed firm Eileson was heading.

Eileson had been on the way to the *Nanuk* in the company of another airplane, which was forced to turn back due to fog over the Bering Sea. It seemed Eileson became another casualty of the weather.

A rescue effort was immediately started by the Soviet government and Avco, the parent company of Alaska Airways, but its organization

Russell Merrill, in his cabin Travelair, is about to fly some hunters off the mudflats at Cook Inlet to hunting grounds around Rainy Pass. Merrill disappeared in this airplane shortly after this flight.

to the remote area in the dead of winter proved so cumbersome that 40 days went by without any aircraft arriving on the scene. The vanished fliers had emergency rations for only 30 days.

The official pace of the rescue finally got to Eileson's anxious bush pilot colleagues. They couldn't stand waiting for the right conditions and the arrival by sea of crated rescue aircraft that were more capable than their fleet. In mid-December, during a raging snowstorm, Joe Crosson and Harold Gillam stuffed a Waco and a Stearman, both open-cockpit biplanes, with emergency supplies and headed for the *Nanuk*. Gillam, who had earned his pilot license only the year before and had only 40 hours of flying time and one cross-country flight under his belt, was following the more experienced Crosson. They made it across to a Siberian village before they were forced down by the storm for the night.

The next day they set out again, but lost each other in the blinding blizzard. Crosson returned with difficulty to the village, but Gillam never arrived. An anxious and dejected Crosson made it alone to the *Nanuk* the following day only to find Gillam's Stearman parked next to the ship. The determined novice barged blindly through the storm on a compass course and pulled off a feat of perfect navigation. He was on his way to becoming a legend for getting through when everyone else was grounded.

The weather was so foul that Crosson and Gillam were able to search for only eight days over the next five weeks. Others joined the search, including Soviet and Canadian aircraft, but Crosson and Gillam finally spotted the wreck as they headed back to Alaska to pick up more gasoline. It took another three weeks to find the bodies in the rock-hard snowdrifts. By the time it was over, Avco spent more than $500,000 on the rescue effort.

The Second Oldest Surviving Airplane

The Stearman that Gillam flew had barely been in Alaska for a year but already had an interesting past. It was brought into the territory by the Arctic Prospecting and Development Company and promptly sent on its first flight to Walker Lake, about 80 miles northwest of Bettles, beyond the

Harold Gillam arrives in an open cockpit Stearman at the icebound fur ship *Nanuk* about 600 miles from Nome to search for Ben Eileson and Earl Borland who disappeared on a fur retrieval flight. Gillam and Joe Crosson, who flew in a Waco, were joined by other search aircraft. It took them a month and a half to find the lost fliers who had died instantly in the crash.

Harold Gillam had the nerves to go with the fur fashion statement and steely face and made a name for himself as the Territory's most capable bad weather flier. He was willing to fly and able to get through when everyone else passed on a trip because of the weather.

Fairchild 71

Year Introduced: 1932
Engine: 420 horsepower Pratt & Whitney Wasp Jr.
Fuel: 160 gallons
Gross weight: 6,000 pounds
Payload (with full fuel): 1,000 pounds
Seats: 7
Cruise Speed: 95 miles per hour
Highlights: An early workhorse of the bush with excellent high altitude performance, it pioneered glacier landings.

Arctic Circle where the Gates of the Arctic National Park is today. Upon landing, it crashed and was severely damaged. What happened next is another typical can-do tale of bush flying.

When Noel Wien heard of the accident, he snapped up the wreck, sight unseen, for $3,500 and flew up to inspect it. The biplane's lower wings were both totaled. Wien immediately created a set of templates with scissors, paper, and pencil for every single component of the destroyed wings. He flew the templates to Fairbanks where a carpentry shop used the templates to make a new pair of wings. Wien's brother, Ralph, and mechanic Earl Borland flew the completed wings back to the wreck on the frozen lake. They bolted them on and flew the airplane home.

The Stearman went on to many more adventures (and crashes) and today it hangs in the Alaska Aviation Heritage Museum on Lake Hood. It's the second oldest surviving airplane in Alaska.

The Ill-Fated MacAlpine Expedition

While the search was on for Eileson and Borland, another highly publicized, marathon rescue was underway in Canada's Northwest Territories to find what Canadians came to call "the ill-fated MacAlpine Expedition."

In the summer of 1929, Colonel C. D. H. MacAlpine, president of the Dominion Explorer's Club and backer and companion of Punch Dickins on the first flight across the Barrens, organized another 4,000-mile aerial exploration of Canada's then largely uncharted Northwest Territories. In two aircraft, the eight-member expedition planned to fly up to Hudson Bay and across the Northwest Territories beyond the Arctic Circle via the Bathurst Inlet to Aklavik near the Alaskan border, where one of the greatest rivers, the MacKenzie, spills into the Arctic Ocean, and then into the Yukon Territory before swinging down home. They hoped to complete the trip in three weeks.

The MacAlpine Expedition departed from Winnipeg, Manitoba, in August in two float-equipped planes, a Fairchild 71 owned by the Explorers Club and a Fokker Universal of Western Canada Airways. Early in the expedition they lost the Fokker at Churchill. It was poorly secured for the night and was swept out by the tide into Hudson Bay and sank. Colonel MacAlpine convinced Western Canada Airways to send a replacement. The next communication via a Hudson Bay Company radio link reported the expedition en route to Bathurst Inlet. That was the last contact from the expedition.

Weeks passed, the return date came and went, and Canada's most massive aerial rescue mission was mounted to find the expedition. A fleet of search planes relocated to Baker Lake north of Churchill, Manitoba, to search the route to Bathurst Inlet. In the meantime, Punch Dickins made three lengthy forays over the rest of the expedition's planned route and covered

A rare restored Fairchild shows the vibrant liveliness of the aircraft of these era in vivid color, which is sometimes hard to sense from period black and white photographs.

"A bushplane crew is a pilot and mechanic who are ready and willing to take any kind of a load to any destination, on or off the map, within the limits of their aircraft and the financial resources of the customer."

—Punch Dickins

thousands of miles in his single-engine plane in subzero temperatures over hostile terrain. The rest of the searchers were plagued by poor weather and mechanical problems and hampered by ice floes as winter approached. At one point they were grounded by the forming ice and they had to wait for the lakes to fully freeze so they could switch to operating on skis. In spite of the difficulties, they managed to scour more than 300,000 square miles of the most likely area where the aircraft could have gone down.

The aerial rescue failed to find the expedition in spite of spending $400,000 and more than two months on the search, but there was a happy ending. In early November, the MacAlpine Expedition staggered into a Hudson Bay Company outpost in Cambridge Bay, northwest of Bathurst Inlet, after an arduous cross-country trek led by a group of Inuit.

The MacAlpine Expedition had flown for hours above a nearly solid layer of fog and clouds and missed Bathurst Inlet. At their estimated time of arrival, nearly out of fuel, they let down through a hole in the fog. They landed at an Inuit winter hunting camp on a lake shore, which they assumed to be the inlet. Afterward, they realized they were more than 100 miles off course to the northwest and were trapped by their fuel status and the rapidly freezing water.

They were completely cut off from the world. Their only way out was a tough slog to Cambridge Bay, but they had to wait for weeks until open water near the bay froze enough to safely cross on foot. They settled in for a long stay and were relatively well equipped to withstand exposure to the weather, but their food supplies ran perilously low and the trek took a severe toll on their dangerously weakened constitutions.

A rescue fleet alighted on skis on Cambridge Bay to fly the emaciated explorers home. The return flight was plagued by a series of technical mishaps and crashes that required the pilots to temporarily abandon the airplanes and some of their occupants and circle back to retrieve them in stages. In the end, rescued and rescuers were all home safely by Christmas.

The Fairchild 71 and 51, originally designed as high altitude camera platforms for Sherman Fairchild's aerial mapping business in the 1920s had all the desirable traits of a bushplane. A high lift wing, powerful engine, large payload capacity, and good handling characteristics made them favorites with bush pilots for over 25 years.

The Risks of Bush Flying

The spate of tragedies in Alaska and the agonies of the MacAlpine Expedition in Canada were sobering reminders of how grim and sparse the options could be for bush pilots if anything went wrong on their remote, exposed routes.

The accidents and the dramatic newspaper headlines that followed distorted the trend in bush flying, but by the late 1920s the odds of staying safe while bush flying were slowly improving. Technological progress was beginning to transform the business, and the pioneering bush pilots were already benefiting from it. Their tenuous experiments with a few dozen aircraft slowly turned into a predictable, reliable, and sustainable form of transportation that grew rapidly and became an indispensable feature of life in the wilderness.

This crew unloads its sleeping bags and sparse supplies and equipment from a Canadian Fairchild a couple of hundred miles from the nearest signs of human existence and may happily subsist for weeks at a time in splendid isolation, an experience that today can only be recreated artificially.

A key development was the creation of a more reliable and powerful air-cooled engine, the Wright Whirlwind. Developed under a U.S. Navy research contract by Charles Lawrence, it was commercialized by Wright as the 200-horsepower J-4. It was soon followed by more powerful versions, as well as similar engines introduced by competing manufacturers, such as the Pratt & Whitney Wasps and Hornets.

These engines were a breakthrough in two important respects. They weighed less and put out as much as twice the power of their predecessors and significantly increased the maximum loads an aircraft could carry. Thanks to advances in metallurgy and the engines' air-cooled simplicity, they were much more reliable than the earlier, mostly liquid-cooled engines. The best advertisement for the Whirlwind's reliability was the 33.5 hours Charles Lindbergh spent behind one on his nonstop flight from New York to Paris in 1927.

The new engines increased the performance of traditional open-cockpit biplanes such as the Waco and the Stearman that Crosson and

Joe Crosson looks out from his Fairchild 71 at Jerry Jones in the Stearman C2 near the Muldrow Glacier on Mt. McKinley in 1932 during the first experiment with landing climbers and scientists on the mountain and keeping them supplied.

For Inuit villagers, the arrival of the bushplane meant year-round contact with the rest of the world instead of three or four times a year. They gave aviary nicknames to this wondrous new phenomenon and called one of the Wien brothers airplanes *Moose Ptarmigan*.

Gillam flew to search for Eileson, but they also made the larger, enclosed-cabin Hamilton monoplane, in which Eileson was lost, possible.

Among the airplanes equipped with the new engines, the ones that pointed the way to the future of bush flying were the Fairchild series of single-engine high-wing monoplanes introduced in the late 1920s. They were created by Sherman Fairchild, a Long Island-based inventor who practically monopolized aerial mapping and went into the aircraft business because he couldn't find a suitable airplane for Fairchild Aerial Surveys.

Fairchild needed an enclosed cabin to protect his camera crews from the elements, the ability to carry a heavy load to haul their equipment, a high-lift wing to quickly get them to high altitudes, and a stable platform for their cameras. Given the remote locations and varied conditions under which Fairchild Aerial Mapping did its work, the airplanes also had to be able to operate on floats, skis, and wheels. The Fairchilds were among the first versatile cabin-class monoplanes and bush pilots quickly noticed they were tailor-made for their own needs.

Jungle Airlift

An airlift that occurred in 1932 half a world away in the steaming jungles of New Guinea far superseded the achievements of Western Canada Airways' 1925 airlift that hauled drilling equipment in Fokker Universals to Fort Churchill on Hudson Bay. The aircraft used in this airlift were Junkers G-31 Trimotors, the forerunner of the Junkers 52. Their task was to transport a massive dredge to the Bulolo goldfield in the mountains for Bulolo Gold Dredging from the coastal town of Lae. There was no other option to get the dredge to the site, which was accessible only on foot. Three G-31s took part in the airlift and were all operated by Pard Mustar's Guinea Airways. One was owned by the airline and the other two were bought by Bulolo Gold specifically for the project. Mustar, one of Australia's most famous bush pilots, and his airline were ideal for the job. They had been flying for the New Guinea gold fields since 1927.

The powerful, high-lift G-31s, which could lift 3 1/2 tons to 8,000 feet in 12 minutes and maintain a positive climb rate at gross weight on two engines, managed the dredge parts with ease on the 40-mile hop across the

Eight of these dredges were airlifted into the Bulolo goldfields by the G-31s. Note the size of the man in the lower left.

6,000-foot ridges into the valley behind them where the airstrip was at 3,200 feet. Their crowning achievement was delivering the dredge's two largest parts, each of which weighed 7,000 pounds. By contrast, the largest piece carried on the airlift to Fort Churchill by the Fokkers weighed 600 pounds.

In 1942, the four G-31s were destroyed by Japanese bombers and the gold field airlift came to an end. By then, they had airlifted 40,259 tons to the mines, including a total of eight dredges. It was a stunning achievement considering that in 1931, the entire U.S. airline industry had carried only 513 tons of cargo.

Eight of these dredges were airlifted into the Bulolo goldfields by the G-31s. Note the antlike size fo the man in the lower right.

Joe Crosson was in a muscular, 450-horsepower Fairchild 71 when he was Alaska's first pilot to land on a glacier. He set it down on the Muldrow Glacier on Mt. McKinley in April 1932. Crosson's first detailed sortie around Mt. McKinley, also in the Fairchild, had been two years earlier to assess the potential of aerial sightseeing around the mountain. He was commissioned by the McKinley Tourist and Transportation Company to fly its general manager, the governor of Alaska, and a handful of other officials on an exploratory sightseeing flight. He piled them into the Fairchild's seven passenger seats on a perfect day and enthralled them for more than three hours exploring the mountain and its vicinity at 9,000 feet.

Mt. McKinley was beginning to draw mountaineering and scientific expeditions by this time. Airplanes often flew over to check on the expeditions. People and supplies could be placed at base camps high up on the mountain by air in about an hour instead of spending grueling weeks by dogsled and on foot from staging points more than 100 miles away. Glacier surfaces could be treacherous, however, even for climbers. Nobody knew if airplanes could safely deal with the crevasses, snowdrifts, and other hazards they posed. Joe Crosson found out on April 25, 1932, when his Fairchild 71, loaded with cargo and three apprehensive mountaineers, approached Muldrow Glacier at 5,600 feet and made a perfect landing.

The departure didn't go nearly as well. In fact, it didn't go at all. A storm materialized with notorious swiftness and Crosson rushed to beat it. On his takeoff run, lengthened by the high altitude's thin air, he managed to get airborne in the swirling snow, but a downdraft slammed the Fairchild back on the ice. Crosson was barely able to come to a stop before he hit rough terrain. He was stuck in the raging storm. He didn't want to abandon his airplane, but self-preservation finally forced him to struggle the 3 miles on foot in near whiteout conditions back to base camp.

Bob Reeve perfected glacier flying out of Valdez, Alaska, to the nearby mines located in practically inaccessible terrains. Here he has landed his Fairchild 51 at the Big Four Mine at 6,000 feet on the Brevier Glacier.

One of Alaska Southern Airways' Lockheed Vegas was the first aircraft to provide regular air service in southeast Alaska and began in 1929. It is pictured at the seaplane dock at Juneau in this colorized period photo.

The next day, in clear weather, the Fairchild lifted off for home after a punishing takeoff run across hard frozen snow ridges. Within a week it was back, this time accompanied by the Stearman that the Wiens had rebuilt on Walker Lake. The resupply mission went smoothly on a calm, sunny day.

Several days later, they received news of the death of two expedition members, claimed by a crevasse, and the critical condition from altitude sickness of another mountaineer. Nothing could be done for the dead, but the Stearman had the sick mountaineer back in Fairbanks within five hours for a full recovery, an unheard of rescue of someone stranded high on a glacier.

The Stearman made one more glacier landing but broke an axle on touchdown and had to have the Fairchild drop the necessary parts for the repairs before it could safely depart. The Stearman's pilot communicated with the Fairchild by writing his messages in the snow with lampblack.

Although these glacier landing experiments were successful, they were risky, and airplanes stayed away from McKinley's slopes for some time to come. In an even wilder corner of Alaska, a pilot named Bob Reeve made glacier landings such an important part of his business that he became known as the Glacier Pilot.

Reeve's Fairchild makes a routine delivery of mining equipment at the Ruff and Tuff mine on the Columbia Glacier.

The Glacier Pilot

Reeve had stowed away on a ship to Alaska in early 1932, penniless after squandering his sizable savings from flying for Pan American Grace Airlines up and down the length of South America for the previous two years. In Valdez he found a totaled Alexander Eaglerock biplane, ancient even by the standards of the day, and agreed to rebuild it if the owner let him rent it afterward to start an air service. Nestled on the coast amidst the mineral-rich Chugach Range, Valdez is surrounded by some of the most inaccessible terrain in Alaska. The easily reachable claims had already been exploited around Valdez, but lack of practical access held up prospectors and miners from working the higher elevations deeper in the mountains. Reeve and his air service found a ready clientele.

While the ancient, anemic open-cockpit Eaglerock wasn't the ideal airplane for the job, Reeve flew it ragged and managed to scrape together enough income to acquire a Fairchild 51. A 300-horsepower scaled-down version of the Fairchild 71, it had the performance for the high altitudes that held the miners' interests. More often than not, the only places to land in this hostile terrain were on its innumerable glaciers.

This is Alaska Southern Airways' luggage label featuring the allure of Alaska and the Vegas the airline used.

The Alaska Coastal Airlines Vega is at the Juneau dock with the steamship Baranoff.

The Juneau dock continues to be a bustling center of floatplane activity. Ships still dock right next to the planes as they have been for three-quarters of a century. The Juneau gold mine, visible above the Vega's cowling (in the top photo), is in ruin, but the new gold mine for the floatplanes are the cruise ships and their tens of thousands of passengers keen to go flightseeing.

Bob Reeve's first glacier landing was over before he realized it. He flew a prospector to Big Four, a mineral claim 6,000 feet high on the Brevier Glacier, and set up an approach. As he throttled back and anticipated the touchdown, there was a sudden explosion of snow, a deceleration, and then they were still. They had arrived. Reeve experienced the loss of depth perception that plagues pilots landing on fields of snow when there is no horizon or other visual clues to provide any perspective.

On a later flight, Reeve touched down on another glacier, gently rolled out, and routinely left the engine running at idle for a quick turnaround. As he opened the door and stepped out, a hysterical shriek from the back startled the heck out of him. It turned out that his passenger was suffering from a severe case of tricked depth perception. The crusty old miner thought they were still flying and Reeve had gone nuts and was abandoning him in midair.

Following his first tentative arrival on the Brevier Glacier, Reeve hauled practically an entire mining community to the Big Four claim. Among his cargo was an ore crusher, a mill with a casing that weighed half a ton, sorting tables, a compressor, all the equipment and materials to build huts for the miners, diesel engines, and fuel to run the machines and keep the men warm. The economics of this job illustrate why the airplane was indispensable to business in Alaska. Pack animals could have lugged in the equipment, but it would have taken months and cost 35 cents a pound. Reeve completed the job in a week of flying and charged only 4 cents a pound.

Reeve also managed to provide year-round service on skis to the high country in spite of the fact that Valdez was at sea level and free of snow and ice for the summer. He discovered that when there was no snow the skis worked just fine on the oozing, slimy tidal mudflats around Valdez when the tide was out—an ingeniously simple, if messy, bush pilot solution.

In coming years, Reeve and a modestly growing fleet of his airplanes hauled as much as 1,500 tons of equipment into the high mining country of the Chugach to scores of claims with such evocative names as Rough and Tough, Little Giant, Mayfield, and Gibraltar.

Rise to Fame

Reeve came to the outside world's attention when he agreed to fly famed mountaineer and explorer Bradford Washburn and his three-member team to their base camp at 8,500 feet on Walsh Glacier in the Yukon. From here the party planned to climb the then still-unscaled 17,150-foot Mt. Lucania on the immense Saint Elias ice cap. The distance from Valdez was 240 air miles, but Reeve delivered the team, in spite of challenging weather and melting ice late in the season.

Washburn was most impressed by Reeve's final departure under trying conditions following a four-day rainstorm that left the Fairchild with little room for its takeoff run. Reeve considered the odds, firewalled the throttle, and hung on. To Washburn's astonishment, the Fairchild fell off the ridge when it reached its edge and disappeared. Fearing the worst, Washburn was even more amazed to suddenly see the airplane rise like a phoenix from the terrain and fly away. It was a technique Reeve had used before, letting his barely controllable airplane fall off a cliff to gain flying speed. Washburn climbed his mountain and made sure the world knew Bob Reeve's part in it.

Permanent Air Service

The cabin class blossomed during the 1930s on the heels of the Fairchilds. Roomy, powerful aircraft with large load-bearing capabilities came on the market in increasing numbers and could be flown with equal ease on wheels, floats, and skis. The versatility, reliability, and availability of these cabin-class aircraft made large-scale, dependable flying a reality in the bush. Among them were the Lockheed Vega, the Bellanca Pacemaker and Skyrocket, and several models of Stinsons and Wacos.

Ellis Air Transport is open for business in Ketchikan in 1935 with its first cabin Waco. Bob Ellis is standing on the pontoon. The company he started is now part of Alaska Airlines.

The ability of the cabin class to reliably haul a decent load on floats finally brought permanent air service to southeast Alaska's watery world of fog-shrouded islands, glaciers, and icy mountains. Alaska-Washington Airways opened for business with panache when *Juneau*, its Lockheed Vega, touched down on Juneau's Gastineau Channel on April 15, 1929, after a seven-and-a-half-hour nonstop flight from Seattle, Washington. Anscel Eckmann, Alaska-Washington Airways' chief pilot, was at the controls and was accompanied by pilot Robert "Bob" Ellis who acted as navigator on the flight and became one of southeast Alaska's biggest air service operators.

Alaska-Washington Airways operated as many as six Vegas in Alaska over the next two years: the *Juneau*, *Taku*, *Sitka*, *Skagway*, *Wrangell*, and the *Petersburg*. The aircraft were based in Juneau, Ketchikan, Sitka, and Seattle and provided region-wide service. They were the first to connect Alaska to the lower 48 on a schedule. Among the pilots were Eckmann, Ellis, Pat Renahan, and Gene Meyring. One of its mechanics was Gordon Graham, who ranked among Alaska's best-known and longest-serving airplane mechanics.

A Lockheed Vega is in front of the Alaska Air Transport hangar in Juneau. Note the flightseeing advertisement. Alaska Air Transport, founded by Shell Simmons, later merged with Alex Holden's Marine Airways to form Alaska Coastal Airlines which merged with Ellis Air Transport and became part of Alaska Airlines.

45

The Curtiss Robin was a three seat sport aircraft of the 1930s and found a role in the bush with operators who could afford only to start small. A floatplane version was the first aircraft of Tony Schwamm's St. Petersburg Air Service which hired Bill Stedman as an apprentice mechanic and launched him on a flying career that earned him the nickname Mr. Goose thanks to all the time he spent flying the Grumman Goose.

An interesting mission for the Vegas was flying fish trap patrols, an early form of law enforcement. Thievery from the traps was endemic in the region and a significant economic loss to the canneries. When the Vegas appeared out of nowhere over the traps to check the boat registrations, the fish filching decreased sharply.

In spite of a promising start, Alaska-Washington Airways was short lived. A series of crashes caused by weather or mechanical failure put three of its Vegas out of action, and the pressures of the Depression on the airline's southern operations in Seattle put it out of business by 1932. The residents of the southeast took a liking to air service and the remnants of Alaska-Washington Airways were salvaged by a local cannery owner. He bought the three remaining Vegas, hired the men who flew and maintained them, and renamed the venture Alaska Southern Airways. A Fairchild 71 repossessed from a fur smuggler by U.S. Customs and a Loening Commuter based in Cordova joined the Vegas.

Pioneer Airways, another small start-up airline flying two Stinson SM8As, competed with Alaska Southern Airways. Pioneer was run by Roy Jones who was back in the region for a second try after his Curtiss flying boat, the *Northbird*, sank during the summer of 1924 when he was running southeast Alaska's first air service, Northbird Aviation. Jones returned in 1930 with pilot Jim Dodson, an ex-Navy flier who had done a tour on one of America's first aircraft carriers, the *Lexington*. Pioneer Airways wasn't much more fortunate than Jones' earlier venture had been. One of its Stinsons, the *Sea Pigeon*, crashed three times that summer. Dodson was badly injured in one of the crashes. He headed north after he recovered and became one of the Territory's best and well-liked bush pilots.

The other Stinson, called the *Northbird* by Jones for old times' sake, was sold to form Ketchikan Airways, but it seemed to take the company's bad luck along with it. First a hangar collapsed on it and put it out of action for some time. It was repaired and flown by Murrell "Sass" Sasseen, a young mechanic and pilot destined for a long bush-flying career, but he didn't have better luck. The Stinson unceremoniously dumped him in the Gastineau Channel and was totaled because of a control failure. Like Dodson, Sasseen headed north and had a great career.

HS-2L Curtiss Flying Boat

Year Introduced: 1917
Engine: 400 horsepower Liberty
Fuel: 180 gallons
Gross weight: 6,400 pounds
Payload (with full fuel): 800 pounds
Seats: 5
Cruise Speed: 65 miles per hour
Highlights: These military surplus flying boats with challenging handling characteristics demonstrated the utility of the airplane in the wilderness.

Handling the Weather

As the floatplanes gained a toehold in the region, the modest beginnings of one of southeast Alaska's most enduring air services got its start when Shell Simmons, a novice pilot, decided he liked flying better than working in the mines. He struggled to launch his flying career around Juneau with a marginally safe Jenny jury-rigged on a single central float and a tiny two-seat German Klemm monoplane he used to instruct. His break came when he was hired to fly the Panhandle Air Transport Company's sole airplane, *Patco*, an especially powerful Stinson with an oversized engine on Fairchild floats.

Bush fliers in southeast Alaska face an especially great challenge from the frequent, rapidly changing precipitation and fog. Pilots need the special skills that Simmons and his contemporaries pioneered on flights like a routine run to the Chicagof Mine west of Juneau. Soon after he started to fly *Patco*, Simmons took his first run to that mine. He was confronted with a wall of snow that would cause any prudent outsider to turn tail but would make the airplane only marginally useful if it so easily scared off local pilots. Simmons slowed down to barely above stall, eased the Vega to within 100 feet of the water, and glued the wing to the barely visible shoreline not much more than a wingspan away. He gained little comfort from the frothing Pacific below the Vega, knowing that unlike the quieter inlets suitable for floatplanes, the stormy open water crashing against the rocky shore might as well be cement in case of an emergency landing.

In time, the snow became so thick that Simmons began to lose the shore. He was close to the southeast bush pilot's limit to flyable weather. Pushing on until suitable, calmer water appeared below, he safely put the Vega down but didn't give up. He slowly taxied the last few miles to the

Fairbanks' Weeks Field was a bustling airport in the 1930s. A lineup of visiting Army bombers is seen in the parking area. Urban growth eventually swallowed up the field, and aviation moved into bigger and better quarters further out of town.

Chicagof Mine.

Ironically the weather almost ended Simmon's career on that flight when he wasn't even in the airplane. High winds blew the aircraft over on its back during the night and it was totaled. The air service's owners threw in the towel and Simmons was out of a job. Others may have given up, but he rounded up a group of friends, bought the wreck for $3,000, and had it rebuilt. When he brought it back from Seattle in the summer of 1935, it was painted in the blue and yellow livery of Alaska Air Transport, his brand new airline. A Bellanca Pacemaker, a Fairchild 71, and a Lockheed Vega soon joined the fledgling airline.

Simmons benefited in an indirect way from the interest outsiders paid to developments in Alaskan aviation. By the mid-1930s Pan American's visionary founder, Juan Trippe, realized his globe-encircling dreams with extensive operations throughout South America and flying boat service to the Pacific. Eyeing the future potential of the Alaskan air bridge to the Far East and noting aviation's growing importance in Alaska itself, Pan American acquired Alaska Airways and several other smaller operators in 1935, including Simmons' competitor, Alaska Southern Airways. The new venture was called Pacific Alaska Airways (PAA), which became a subsidiary of Pan Am and featured the PAA winged globe logo in its livery. Alaska Airways' Joe Crosson was its general manager.

This development appeared to be a serious competitive threat to the smaller operators, but within a year Pacific Alaska Airways completely pulled out of local bush operations in the southeast to concentrate on connecting Alaska's main towns with each other and with the United States via Seattle. Simmons suddenly had the local business largely to himself. However, the ex-PAA pilots, including Bob Ellis, who wanted to remain in the area, were out of a job. Ellis decided that if he had to go back to flying on a financial shoestring, it might as well be his own. He managed to assemble a small group of local backers and launched Ellis Air Transport with a cabin-class Waco based in Ketchikan.

Other operators, such as Alex Holden's Marine Airways, also made significant contributions, but Ellis Air Transport in Ketchikan and Simmons' Alaska Air Transport in Juneau became the main players in coming years and each acquired its share of smaller competitors along the way. Although they were intensely competitive, they merged amicably in 1962 and eventually became part of today's Alaska Airlines.

In the meantime, Frank Barr quietly decided to go against the grain and fly on wheels in the southeast float country. As his regular route along the mines between Juneau and Atlin, British Columbia, via the Taku inlet modestly prospered, he acquired a big, stocky Fairchild Pilgrim in 1935. The Pilgrim was designed as an airliner but was quickly overshadowed by more modern aircraft. It had a considerably higher load-bearing capability than aircraft on floats in relation to its size and operating costs. Its price was also right, which made it popular with Alaskan bush-flying services.

Barr could legally pack 2,000 pounds or nine passengers into his 575-horsepower Pilgrim and had acceptable landing spots along his route except for Juneau, where he solved the problem by flying off the tidal sand flats close to where the town's modern airport is today.

A favorite stop for Barr along the Taku River was Mary Joyce's Lodge, a popular resort. Joyce was a feisty Alaskan who dabbled with airplanes and had mushed part of the way to Fairbanks with a team of huskies to attend a beauty contest as Miss Juneau. One winter Barr was snowed in at the lodge for three weeks and was stuck on wheels when the weather cleared. He had no way to get the Pilgrim's skis to the lodge, so he built two open crates out of scrap wood, plopped them under the wheels, and hoped that as the airplane became airborne, the crates would fall away and stay on the ground. The scheme worked perfectly. Today Taku River Lodge draws thousands of day visitors, flown in on big, radial-engine floatplanes for a delicious Alaskan salmon barbecue, and for those in the know, perhaps an occasional glimpse of the ghosts of Frank Barr and Mary Joyce.

The Essential Business Tool

The 1930s saw a dramatic expansion of bush flying throughout the rest of Alaska. The appearance of the more capable cabin-class airplanes set off a proliferation of small, individual operators forever locked in cutthroat competition. In time, their chronically tenuous financial condition, created by the constant struggle to outbid each other, led to an inevitable series of consolidations that created the air services that endured. But there would never be a shortage of new entrants to try their luck with a plane, a belief in themselves, and an insatiable desire to fly.

It was common knowledge that an airplane could cover in an hour what it would take a dogsled to cover in a week. Mac McGee varied the theme in his compelling advertising copy and summed up how the airplane changed the wilderness.

Fur trading was only one of Mac McGee's many interests and reasons for acquiring an airplane. McGee Airways soon grew into a fleet of eight aircraft. Long before the modern major air carriers spent a mint on learned studies about the merits of single0type fleets, McGee's common sense told him all he needed to know about the advantages of fleet commonality.

49

A Star Airlines Bellanca Pacemaker is pictured in the Chugach mountains in 1933. Star Airlines merged with McGee Airways when Mac McGee wanted to move on to other business ventures. He retained the right to return and take charge in case of financial problems. McGee came back several times to guide the airline business.

An increasing number of aviation boosters of the 1930s viewed the airplane as an essential business tool. Among them was Linious "Mac" McGee, an adventurer who arrived in Alaska as a stowaway on a ship and became a respected mining entrepreneur and fur trader. McGee amassed a lot of pelts on his fur-buying trips and decided the only way to transport them efficiently was by his own private airplane. He joined with a former barnstormer and they bought a Stinson SM8A from Varney Airlines, a forerunner of United Airlines, and hit the trapper trails. From the beginning, McGee planned to offer his airplane for the use of others. He bought another Stinson, and McGee Airways was on its way.

McGee Airways soon operated seven Stinsons, for McGee was an early believer that standardization resulted in great operating efficiencies and less cost. He put his pilots on a commission and paid them 12.5 percent of the fee generated by any flight they sold. Among the men who flew for him was Oscar Winchell, a cowboy turned bush pilot who became known throughout Alaska as the Flying Cowboy.

In addition to well-established Alaska Airways, which had recently acquired a small operator called Pacific International Airways and became Pacific Alaska Airlines when it was acquired by Pan America Airways in 1934, McGee faced competition mostly from Star Air Service. Star was founded by Steve Mills and Jack Waterworth with the backing of Earl Dunkle, an engineer and superintendent of the Lucky Shot Mine in the nearby Cugach Mountains. The company started operations with one open-cockpit Fleet biplane, primarily to provide flight instruction, but soon had a fleet of eight aircraft, including several Bellancas that served mostly along the Kuskokwim River. McGee Airways concentrated primarily on the business around Bristol Bay, but both companies struggled financially and McGee was more interested in focusing on his mining interests once again.

A deal was struck and McGee sold his airline to Star Air Service and agreed to give the new venture a sizable loan to seal the transaction. The combined operation had 15 airplanes and was renamed Star Air Lines, but it wasn't the end of its association with McGee. The wily businessman stipulated that if his loan wasn't repaid on schedule, he could return to put the airline back in financial shape, which was a task he performed more than once over the next few years.

Up in Fairbanks, Alaska Airways had most of the business. One of their pilots was Noel Wien. He had agreed not to compete with Alaska Airways for a set time when he sold them his Nome operation and returned to fly for them until their agreement ran out in late 1932. As soon as the contract expired, he was back in business on his own, with an agile 300-horsepower Bellanca Pacemaker.

Wien launched his new airline with a single airplane and successfully competed with Alaska Airways because he was a legend throughout Alaska and more customers clamored to fly with him than he could accommodate. While the income the Bellanca brought in provided a living, it wasn't

This is one of 11 Pilgrims that flew in Alaska for years. The one in the Alaska Aviation Heritage Museum retired in 1985 after it hauled a million pounds of salmon as a fish freighter based in Bristol Bay. It is one of only four aircraft on the National Register.

It wasn't all work and no play even in the earliest and brutal days of flying the bush. Fishing and hunting parties always formed an important part of the bush services' business as sportsmen were among the first to grasp how much more they could experience in the little time they had for their recreational interests.

enough to acquire additional aircraft. Wien's chance to expand his business was made possible, ironically, by the deaths of America's most popular radio personality, Will Rogers, and around-the-world record pilot Wiley Post, when their Lockheed Vega crashed on takeoff at Barrow, America's northernmost community.

The Rogers-Post tragedy was newsworthy worldwide on the scale of today's space shuttle disasters. The first newspaper to run photographs of the crash would claim the scoop of the decade and millions of dollars in extra newspaper sales. Two competing news organizations, the International News Service (INS) and Associated Press (AP), both had photographers on the scene and raced to get the gruesome images to the world from beyond the Arctic Circle via Seattle. Both organizations put themselves in the hands of Alaska's bush pilots.

Noel Wien with his Bellanca Pacemaker is shown at Weeks Field in Fairbanks after he re-entered aviation as his own boss in 1932. Wien flew this Pacemaker to Seattle on a pioneering flight along an inland route to Seattle over the wildest Canadian Rockies, through the night, bearing the photos of the Wiley Post–Will Rogers crash near Barrow, Alaska. He beat PAA's plane with the rival news service's photos and made enough for his efforts to buy a Ford Trimotor on the spot before flying home.

The race came down to the pilots of Alaska Airways, which had become a Pan American Airways subsidiary. Pacific Alaska Airlines carried the AP's photos and Noel Wien rushed south in his Bellanca for the INS. The PAA had a head start and bettors would have favored it heavily with all its resources and Pan American support. They would have been in for a big shock when Noel Wien arrived in Seattle after 20 hours of practically nonstop flying through the night, and the PAA flight was nowhere to be seen.

Wien took the interior route from Fairbanks to Seattle, which was the first time this difficult

This Wien Air Alaska Ford trimotor Tin Goose was bought from Wein's earnings for flying the Post–Rogers crash photos to Seattle. An ex-Northwest Airlines aircraft, it was a favorite of Noel Wien's and the villagers he served.

option was attempted between the two cities. PAA stuck to its regular route via Juneau and was held up by the southeast's notoriously soggy weather. The interior route ran to the east of Alaska's Coastal Mountains, via Whitehorse in the Yukon, and down through British Columbia, roughly the way the Alaska Highway would run. In the 1930s, this was one of the most remote, hostile, and least explored areas of North America, where discovery and rescue was unlikely even if Wien would have managed to pull off a night crash landing in case of trouble.

Conservative, unhurried, taciturn Noel Wien, who often remained on the ground when the more foolhardy boldly sailed forth, had gambled and won, although he regarded the flight as just another charter. His reward was a fat paycheck, which he spent to buy a Tin Goose, a big, all-metal, ex-Northwest Airlines Ford Trimotor. It was the biggest airplane to alight on Fairbanks' Weeks Field when Wien proudly flew it home and was a favorite of his in the Wien Air Alaska fleet for years to come.

By the late 1930s, Wien Air Alaska had eight aircraft that covered all of Alaska except the Anchorage area and the southeast. Noel Wien's airline served Nome again, where he had started his first flying service, and his younger brother, Sig, pioneered air service to Barrow. Sig was based in Barrow for years and was a father figure to the town he alone linked with the outside world in the winter when it was too cold to run the dogsleds.

Building a Business

As flying matured in Alaska, a pattern emerged in the division of the available business. The more established, bigger flying services had most of the business based at the larger or geographically more important settlements, such as Anchorage, Fairbanks, and Nome. Bush pilots who gained experience working for others and wanted to start their own flying services found the best opportunities in the smaller settlements to provide feeder services to connect to the bigger hubs.

It was difficult to conjure up the capital for a one-plane service on a bush pilot's salary, and pilots were always on the lookout for innovative opportunities. Jim Dodson, one of the territory's most popular and respected bush pilots, went north from southeast Alaska after his brief stint with short-lived Pioneer Airways, took whatever flying jobs he could find, and received an unusual break in 1934. A dentist from Ruby along the Yukon River who treated the Inuit communities in the area concluded that the best way for him to get around his wide-ranging bush beat was by his own airplane. He bought a Stinson and asked Dodson to fly him on his rounds. In exchange, Dodson could fly the airplane for his own commercial business once he delivered the dentist to a particular village. Because the dentist could stay in a village for weeks before he was done, it was a lucrative opportunity for Dodson and he jumped at it.

Dodson moved his young family to Ruby and threw himself into his work. His wife, Lillian, was left alone with their infant twin sons for weeks at a time. She cheerfully met the challenges of frontier life and brought in frozen diapers off the wash line, 50 at a time, and stacked them like cordwood, while her husband built a business.

On a typical day, Dodson loaded the Stinson with supplies at Ruby, where they were stockpiled by riverboat, and delivered them to a string of mines and villages including Long Creek, Midnight Creek, Greenstone Creek, Poorman, Colorado Creek, Esperanto Creek, Ophir Creek,

This Alaska Southern Airways advertisement is still a popular feature in the waiting rooms of modern bush operators.

Jim and Lillian Dodson are pictured with their first Gullwing Stinson in 1937. Jim Dodson, an ex-Navy pilot, ran his own air service with his wife and operated as many as three Gullwing Stinsons within a few years. In the 1940s, Jim Dodson Airways was one of several smaller operators that merged into Northern Consolidated Airways where Dodson was a senior executive for many years.

Yankee Creek, Takotna, and also down to McGrath and other stops along the Kuskokwim River. It made for long summer days in the land of the midnight sun.

As Dodson's business became more widely known, he moved it to Fairbanks where his family was more comfortable. There his wife could take to the bank the pokes filled with thousands of dollars of gold dust that he flew in for the miners from the field. The pokes were handled with surprising nonchalance. Lillian Dodson tossed them on her car's front seat as she ran her errands in town. But the gold was safe, she later recalled, because the texture and color of each mine's unprocessed gold was unique and so recognizable that even she could tell them apart after a few times, and it could be sold only to the government, which made it difficult to cash in on the contents of a stolen poke.

By 1936, Dodson formed Jim Dodson Air Service with his own Gullwing Stinson, and within a year he had three of them and his own hangar at Weeks Field. He branched out to the north to Beaver, Fort Yukon, and Arctic Village, and eastward to Eagle and Chicken. Most of his clients in this area were fur trappers like Johnny Muskrat, who had ranged as far as Siberia to look for fur long before the airplane arrived in Alaska, but Dodson also flew the occasional reverend on his traveling ministry.

Emergency Flights

As bush-flying services spread throughout the wilderness during the 1930s, medical emergency missions assumed legendary importance. A bush pilot rarely refused a medical emergency flight regardless of the weather, time of day, distance, or the hours already flown that day. Sig Wien and Joe Crosson in Alaska and Wop May and Vic Horner in Canada flew arduous emergency flights in atrocious weather to rush serum to isolated communities to prevent diphtheria epidemics. These flights made national headlines and saved hundreds of lives. Lifesaving medical evacuation flights, although not always widely reported, were no less dramatic and the pilots flying them willingly took risks they wouldn't think of accepting on routine flights.

Few pilots bargained for the experience Jim Dodson had flying a young woman from Ruby to Fairbanks for maternity care. They were flying low and the Stinson was chasing its shadow in the sunlight. Dodson kidded his passenger that the shadow was the stork coming, but the joke was on him when the woman gave birth in flight. Fortunately for Dodson, his wife and a nurse were also along and the event went off without a hitch. A decade later, another in-flight birth happened again to Dodson, but this time it was a wet, turbulent night and he was alone with his pregnant passenger. Nevertheless, it all went well.

Jim Dodson regularly ran this small ad in the Fairbanks papers. This, along with his reputation, was sufficient to attract enough customers to make his flight service a success.

The Weather Challenge

As the airplanes became more reliable, weather was the bush pilots' biggest challenge, and no pilot tackled bad weather as audaciously as Harold Gillam. Alaskans joked that there were three kinds of weather. There was Pan American weather, named after the airline's conservative standards and meticulous adherence to the weather minimum regulations that were put in place by the faraway government aviation bureaucracy. There was Alaska weather: good, bad, and indifferent, and flown by all the bush pilots. Then there was Gillam weather, when everybody grounded himself, except Harold Gillam.

Gruff, short, tight-lipped, and a loner, Gillam was a precise, meticulous pilot. His blind faith in his perceived ability to maintain situational awareness in the worst weather made him immune to the healthy fear every other pilot had of becoming lost and flying into an obstruction. Pilots were intensely competitive, especially when they flew the same route in the same weather, but common sense usually prevailed and no egos were unduly bruised making the go/no go decision in the face of variably gray skies. Gillam saw no shades of gray. If he had a flight scheduled, he blasted off even when the birds cowered on the ground. Paradoxically, his bull-headed attitude took the competitive pressures off his fellow pilots because they considered him imprudent. One pilot used to quip when a storm raged that he wasn't going anywhere because God was too busy taking care of Gillam.

Gillam may have been good, but he was also lucky. He had numerous weather-related close calls, such as breaking out within feet of an obstruction on arrival at a socked-in destination, or running off a runway that loomed out of the fog in the wrong place. Within a year of the formation of Gillam Airways at Chitina to serve the rugged copper mining district southeast of Anchorage,

Gullwing Stinson

Year Introduced: 1937
Engine: 420 horsepower Pratt & Whitney Wasp Jr.
Fuel: 105 gallons
Gross weight: 5,000 pounds
Payload (with full fuel): 600 pounds
Seats: 5
Cruise Speed: 135 miles per hour
Highlights: This elegant, versatile cabin class airplane was designed for general aviation that readily adapted to bush flying. It was valued for its room and speed.

This is a fine portrait of a Gullwing Stinson on skis. The Gullwing Stinson was a glamorous late model cabin class airplane and popular with wealthy private fliers in more genteel surroundings. It was rarely seen on snow, except in bush use.

inland from Cordova, he had six crashes that left him $30,000 in debt. He doggedly flew on and branched out to fly the Kuskokwim, where the inhabitants claimed they could set their watches by the punctuality of his Pilgrim on his lengthy mail runs.

Gillam awed his customers and irked his fellow pilots with his blind willingness to barrel into any blizzard. An admiring third-grade village boy's poem to his hero summed it up and became widely quoted: "He thrill 'em, chill 'em, spill 'em, but no killem Gillam." The odds evevtually caught up with Gillam and he died in early 1943 in a plane crash on a flight from Seattle to Annette Island near Ketchikan in "Gillam" weather.

Gillam brought air service to the isolated coastal town of Cordova (not far from Bob Reeve's operation at Valdez) when he based one of his airplanes there in 1932 and hired M. D. "Kirk" Kirkpatrick to fly it. Kirkpatrick took over the Cordova-based business two years later and formed Cordova Air Service. One of his pilots was Merle Smith, who was nicknamed Mudhole when Bob Reeve saw Smith nosed over in a pool of mud that totally coated him and his airplane.

Bush Flying Progresses in Alaska and Canada

By the end of the 1930s, there were more than 175 airplanes in Alaska that flew out of more than 100 airports and airstrips, in addition to the countless off-airport landing sites chosen as needed. Bush operators began to install ground-to-air radios at their bases and most frequent destinations. They operated them as an informal network of CB radios, rather than an official aviation communications system, and shared weather information, kept tabs on their positions, and most important, radioed for help when forced down.

As bush flying progressed in Alaska, it also made equally impressive strides throughout Canada. The immense size of the Canadian northern wilderness provided an even bigger challenge than Alaska because of the sheer distances involved. But the miners, trappers, government agencies charged with development, and the enterprises that supported them were an enthusiastic client base

Cordova Airport on Eyak Lake was a simple Lakeside shack in 1934. During the summer, aircraft came and went on floats, and they switched to skis in the winter. The aircraft in the foreground is Harold Gillam's rare Zephyr, which is similar in layout to the Travel Air CW with the pilot in an open cockpit aft and the passengers in an enclosed cabin forward. A runway was built at Cordova shortly after this photograph was taken.

for the bush pilots.

By the early 1930s the Ontario Provincial Air Service (OPAS) operated from 17 bases with a fleet of 26 aircraft. Within the OPAS fleet were 14 de Havilland Puss Moth biplanes on floats, which were a very efficient alternative to the HS-2L flying boats for fire patrols. The Moths could also operate on skis, which enabled OPAS to fly year round. This allowed the organization to establish its own flying school at Sioux Lookout during the winter off-season.

OPAS acquired a DH-61 Giant Moth, an airplane of imposing size, especially when it is on floats. The Giant Moth was used for dusting insect-infested forests, a forest management function

This Pacific Alaska Airways Stearman on floats was used by Wiley Post on a hunting trip. Post loved Alaska and bought property there and wanted to settle in the Territory, but the plan was thwarted by his tragic crash.

Cabin Wacos were a popular choice of wealthy sportsman pilots in the mid-1930s, but they were also favored by bush pilots for their roomy cabins.

that was almost impossible to perform effectively before the arrival of airplanes. OPAS was especially proud of its first all-Canadian aircraft, the Vickers Vedette flying boat. The Vedettes were smaller and more capable than the H boats, which were being phased out, and they served as photo platforms for years to come. Another important addition to the fleet were four Hamilton Metalplanes for general cargo and transportation haulage. The metalplane was OPAS' first all-metal aircraft, which was flyable year round on pontoons and skis. OPAS also had its share of Fairchilds, and its major entry into the cabin-class era came with the purchase of 10 Stinson Reliants in 1937.

Breaking the Uranium Monopoly

Private bush-flying firms also made progress and subsisted on a mix of government and private, corporate contracts, and an increasing flow of ad hoc charters from individual prospectors and other private parties. Two major Canadian bush firms emerged: Doc Oaks' Western Canada Airways and Mackenzie Air Service. Western Canada Airways expanded rapidly following the success of its first big job hauling dredging equipment to Hudson Bay. It built a network of local operations sprinkled throughout Canada and opened the first air link between Vancouver and Victoria in British Columbia. This was the first of a web of routes that connected the island communities around Vancouver, a floatplane service that is still going strong in the hands of local operators today because it remains the only fast way to travel in that area.

Western Canada Airways' most famous pilot, Punch Dickins, pioneered more routes to the north and northwest. Dickins was the first to bring mail service to remote places such as Fort Simpson in the Northwest Territories, and he was the first to reach the western Arctic coast by airplane.

Dickins flew in an intense rivalry with his famous contemporary, Wop May, of Commercial Airlines, but not for long. Commercial Airlines' backers fell victim to the Great Depression and the

The Ontario Provincial Air Service bought a large fleet of Puss Moths in the late 1920s. The small, economical aircraft were excellent fire spotters. In the slow winter season they were used to train OPAS pilots.

airline was absorbed by its rival and put Dickins and May on the same side. As Western Canada Airways became more national in character and acquired several smaller competitors, it changed its name to Canadian Airways Limited.

Canadian Airways and Mackenzie Air Service both based their operations in Edmonton, Alberta, which evolved into a major bush-flying base thanks to a pivotal discovery that set off a mining boom to the north of Edmonton into the Northwest Territories during the 1930s. Mackenzie Air Service played a part in setting off the boom and created new opportunities for the entire bush-flying community.

In 1931, Mackenzie's Leigh Brintnell had flown mining engineer Gilbert LaBine to Great Bear Lake, about 1,000 air miles north of Edmonton in the Northwest Territory on the Arctic Circle, where the miner wanted to examine some promising potential gold finds. It is said that Britnell had suggested their landing spot and noticed it on a previous flight. LaBine was following up on an old prospector's report that dated back to 1900. He didn't find gold, but stashed some rocks that glowed in the dark. Further investigation revealed that LaBine had found the largest uranium mine in the world.

LaBine's find set off a two-year mineral rush to Great Bear Lake and brought booming business for Mackenzie Air Service, Canadian Airways, and a handful of smaller operators. When the

This Fairchild pilot discovers the drawbacks of not covering his aircraft's wings on a moist winter night.

rush subsided, the big mining companies remained and continued to steadily expand their activities into the north and northwest and provided the crucial business the bush fliers needed to make it through the Depression.

LaBine's find became the Eldorado Uranium Mine and broke a monopoly held by King Leopold's uranium mines in the Belgian Congo. The Belgians also had a stranglehold on the radium market, refined from uranium and indispensable for medical x-rays, which were just coming into wide use at that time. Bush flying was a key contributor to break the monopoly.

The Eldorado mine produced radium concentrate on site but had to get it out efficiently to be competitive. The choices were a 1,500-mile river journey against the north-flowing current through rapids and swampland, open only a few months a year, or by air to the railhead at Fort McMurray. The air option proved to be the most economic choice, and Mackenzie Air Service got the contract. The *Eldorado Radium Silver Express*, Mackenzie's Bellanca, hauled full loads of radium concentrate out of Port Radium on Great Bear Lake.

With the continuing expansion and the routine ongoing operation of the mines, the bush-flying services moved more than 200 miles north of Edmonton to the railhead at Fort McMurray, which became a gateway to opening up the Northwest Territories and the Yukon to the rest of the country.

The Great Depression

While the big air services had a lock on most of the bush-flying business, Canada also had its own share of ambitious individualists bent on trying their luck, just like so many bush fliers in Alaska. They embodied the attitude of Punch Dickins who summed up the typical bush-flying crew as "a pilot and mechanic, who are ready and willing to take any kind of a load to any destination, on or off the map, within the limits of their aircraft and the financial resources of the customer." What Dickins didn't mention, however, was how hard the crew had to hustle during the 1930s to get a load to carry as the Great Depression deepened. Few hustled more than Grant McConachie of Edmonton, Alberta, and few became more successful.

McConachie, a burly, jovial extrovert, was besotted with flying as a teenager. The son of a Canadian National Railroad official, he scraped together enough money working odd jobs to earn a pilot's license by 1931, but there were few flying jobs at the height of the Great Depression. He was about to board his ship for Shanghai to fly for the Chinese government when his Uncle Harry, a flamboyant, well-to-do wheeler-dealer with no visible means of support, made him a business proposition he couldn't refuse. Uncle Harry would put up the money to buy a Fokker if his nephew returned to Edmonton to fly it.

Within days McConachie was president and sole pilot of Independent Airways and flew its only plane, a used Fokker. All he needed was a steady client or two. Finding that the more established operators had the available business well in hand, McConachie created an opportunity where others had seen none.

He met by chance the president of the Cold Lake Fish Company, which shipped hundreds of thousands of pounds of frozen whitefish to Chicago by rail during the winter from Cold Lake, north of Edmonton. The fishmonger wistfully mentioned he would be able to charge

The de Havilland DH-61 Giant Moth, about four times the size of the diminutive Puss Moth, was one of the biggest single-engined biplanes ever built. OPAS used it to spray insecticide in its forest infestation control program.

An OPAS engineer handcrafts skis for the organization's aircraft for the coming winter. OPAS did many tasks in-house in the early days, but making skis and floats soon became the niches of specialty shops.

Canadian Airways' unusual single-engined Junkers 52 is being refueled and loaded for its next mission at Gold Pine in 1935. Usually a trimotor, this Junkers was equipped with one especially powerful engine and a super efficient four-blade propeller.

much more for fresh fish, but had to freeze the shipments because it took horse-drawn sleds 10 hours or longer to drag the fish from Cold Lake to the railhead at Bonnyville. McConachie pounced. The Fokker could fly the fish to the railhead in 20 minutes. He walked out with a contract to haul 30,000 pounds of whitefish per week for the season, with more to come if the experiment worked.

Flying as much as 240 hours per month, the intrepid 20-something pilot and his peg-legged mechanic made sure their first steady client would be satisfied. McConachie also caught on quickly to the importance of grabbing any opportunistic cargo and soon had a brisk business air freighting groceries and supplies to the Cold Lake settlements on the empty return legs from the railhead.

Contracts with other fish companies followed and over the next five years Independent Airways' growing and varied fleet hauled millions of pounds of fish from the lakes of northern Alberta to the closest railheads. Like most early bush operators, their pilots stretched the definition of their airplanes' load-bearing capabilities to maximize revenue, something they practically had to do to ensure their financial survival.

Ignoring the manufacturers' values, maximum load was defined as the weight with which their aircraft were capable of staggering into the air. De Havilland's manual for the tiny Puss Moth rated its maximum load at 500 pounds, but McConachie and his fellow pilots experimented and found it could just manage 800 pounds. The Fokker was rated at 600 pounds, but they packed it with 1,200 pounds. To their delight, the large Ford Trimotor they had acquired, rated at 2,000 pounds, could actually wallow aloft with a whopping 3,600 pounds. It was a long time before the regulators caught up with the ways of the bush.

Two HS-2Ls, a Bellanca Pacemaker, and two Puss Moths meet at an Ontario OPAS base in the 1930s. By then the venerable H boats had been in service for over a decade. Note the fuel drum stash.

While small flying services like McConachie's struggled to eke out a living flying fish and hauling small-time prospectors for a pittance, they sometimes snared more lucrative contracts and expanded their business for a surprising reason: the desire for secrecy among prospectors and miners on the trail of a hot claim. In the midst of one of his fish-flying contracts, McConachie was discretely approached by a wealthy gold prospector who wanted himself and his mining crew flown to a claim deep in the Stickine Range, a particularly rugged and remote stretch of British Columbia.

McConachie only had his Puss Moth available for the job and suggested the availability of more suitable aircraft with one of his bigger competitors, but the miner wouldn't hear of it. There were too many ears, eyes, and loose lips at the big outfits that flew for the big mining companies who would be keenly interested in his secret travels. The Puss Moth did just fine and McConachie received instructions to the exact location only when they reached Takla Lake about 500 miles west of Edmonton, where they stashed gasoline. The secret claim was 90 miles beyond the lake.

Their destination turned out to be Two Brothers Lake at an elevation of 5,000 feet, which left the tiny Puss Moth gasping for air amidst the towering, desolate peaks. McConachie duly ferried in the mining party and their supplies in seven flights and headed back to Edmonton with a promise to return in June. He was the only one who knew where the miners were. If anything happened to him by June when the miners' supplies ran out, they would be abandoned and likely perish before they reached civilization. But the risk was worth it to them for the sake of secrecy, and it paid off big time for the miners and McConachie's growing business.

The next spring McConachie was back on Takla Lake with three Fokkers that flew in more than 100 tons of equipment to the Two Brothers Mine, including a sawmill, caterpillar tractor, and a placer mining machine. For the next two summers, the Fokkers ran a lucrative shuttle to the mine.

The prospectors' obsessive secrecy about their destinations may have been well founded, but sometimes it led to tragic results. When Paddy Burke, one of Canada's best-known early bush pilots, vanished with two companions in a Junkers F-13 somewhere over northern British Columbia, they weren't found for a month and a half, mostly because nobody knew exactly where they were going. They were on a flight with a prospector to a claim at a secret location. The massive, frustrating rescue operation claimed the life of famed Alaska-Washington Airlines pilot Pat Renahan and two companions in a Lockheed Vega. When another aircraft finally stumbled on the lost Junkers in late November on the frozen Laird River near the British Columbia-Yukon border, it was four days too

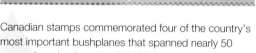

Canadian stamps commemorated four of the country's most important bushplanes that spanned nearly 50 years of service from the first H boats to the Beaver.

Here is a comfortable wilderness lair typical of experienced bush dwellers. They could be prospectors, surveyors, forestry officials, or scientists, and all share the knowledge of living off the land for extended periods back to before the time of bushplanes. For them, the bush plane meant unimaginable luxury. Note the clothes drying on the wing strut and the stovepipe sticking out of the tent.

Flying Doctors

A particularly Australian contribution to the utility of bush flying is the Flying Doctor Service. The challenges of delivering medical services to Australia's farms and ranches in its sparsely settled 2 million-square-mile Outback raised the temptation to use airplanes for the purpose ever since they showed up down under. There were quite a few ad hoc medical flights during the 1920s, but it was useless without a timely way to summon it from hundreds of miles in the bush. Organized service had to wait until a reliable pedal-powered radio was designed in the late 1920s specifically for outback communications. Founded by John Flynn, a Presbyterian missionary, the Flying Doctor Service was launched in 1928 from Cloncurry, Queensland, with Dr. St. Vincent Welch, its first full-time physician, and a de Havilland DH-50 supplied by Qantas and flown by Arthur Affleck, one of its first pilots.

In the early days, off-airport landings were the rule. Whenever Affleck flew into Urrandangie, he landed on the main street and could taxi to any of the settlement's homes, or the local pub, his preferred choice. Nurses were not on the flights until 1960, so pilots often acted as impromptu anesthesiologists under the guidance of surgeons performing emergency operations, often by kerosene lights. The pilot had to be careful not to overdose the patient with ether and had to prevent a buildup of ether fumes around the open flames to prevent an explosion. A 3 a.m. take-off to head for home after such a night was pure relief. Most patients practically worshipped the service, but on rare occasions they could be irreverent. One example is a man who was speared in an altercation. When the spear's handle had to be broken to get the tip out, he complained that the doctor had ruined a perfectly good spear.

An Australian Flying Doctor Service Nomad, built in small numbers for bush use, lands on a stretch of road to evacuate injured victims of a car crash.

Today the service has a fleet of turboprops throughout the Outback on more than a dozen bases. They make more than 6,000 emergency flights a year to evacuate seriously ill patients to the hospital and fly doctors on routine clinical rounds. There are also the occasional mercy flights, where the consequences of their actions are a matter of immediate life or death. On those flights, they are absolved of following all rules and regulations to the best of their judgment. They are free to land off-airport, tackle the weather as they see fit, and take any other risk they are willing to accept to save their patient.

late for Paddy Burke, who had died of exposure.

The odds of avoiding tragedies like the one that claimed the life of Paddy Burke slowly improved as Canadian bush fliers, like Alaskans, embraced the new, more capable cabin-class aircraft and technological advances such as the radio. As the 1930s came to an end, a small group of Canadians made a major technical contribution of their own and created the Noorduyn Norseman, the first aircraft designed explicitly for bush flying.

Canadians made a major technical contribution of their own and created the Noorduyn Norseman, the first aircraft designed explicitly for bush flying.

Bob Noorduyn, the Dutch-born designer of the Norseman, spent years with several British aircraft makers before he joined Fokker in the United States in 1920, followed by stints at Bellanca and Pitcairn. As many of the airplanes he worked on were put in service by bush operators, he saw firsthand that airplanes not explicitly designed for the bush all fell short of meeting the harsh demands of wilderness flying in some respect. In 1934 he moved to Montreal and formed Noorduyn Aircraft Limited to remedy the situation.

Noorduyn's design specifications identified all the key issues of concern to the bush pilot. The aircraft had to have substantial load-bearing capability. Its cabin had to be rapidly convertible between cargo and passenger configurations and its access had to allow for loading large, bulky items. The airplane had to be able to operate on pontoons, skis, and wheels. It also had to perform short takeoffs and landings with a rapid climb rate. The aircraft had to be able to cruise at a fast air speed to get the job done efficiently, but it also had to be capable of slow flight at a suitably low air speed to allow the pilots to safely troll around in marginal visibility. It had to have a substantial range to cope with Canada's vast distances. It had to be easily maintainable in the field with a minimum of basic tools. Last, the cockpit had to be insulated and separate from the main cabin so that pilots wouldn't have to squeeze around a full load to board and not be trapped by cargo in case of an emergency.

The result was a fat-looking high-wing monoplane that lived up to expectations in every respect after a few teething problems were solved, which are normal for every design. The Norseman had a fabric-covered wood wing mated to an exceptionally strong fabric-covered welded steel tube fuselage. As with all aircraft, weight control was key to achieving its ambitious performance goals, and this airframe design provided the lightest option and retained the requirement for easy field repairs.

Junkers 34

Year Introduced: 1926
Engine: 425 horsepower Pratt & Whitney Wasp
Fuel: 108 gallons
Gross weight: 6,600 pounds
Payload (with full fuel): 1,700 pounds
Seats: 10
Cruise Speed: 90 miles per hour
Highlights: It's an excellent early bushplane with great load bearing ability. The last one was in service in Canada until 1962. A drawback at dockside was its low wing.

Noorduyn Norseman Mark IV

Year Introduced: 1936
Engine: 550/600 horsepower Pratt & Whitney Wasp
Fuel: 180 gallons
Gross weight: 6,450 pounds
Payload (with full fuel): 1,500 pounds
Seats: 10
Cruise Speed: 140 miles per hour
Highlights: Thoughtfully designed, especially for the bush, it had a large, roomy cabin and good load bearing. Over 1,600 were built, and were also used for the military. It was the prime bushplane of the 1950s and 1960s.

The Noorduyn Norseman, the first purpose designed bushplane, could carry a hefty external load. Norsemen first entered service in 1936.

STOL (Short Take Off and Landing) aircraft. Its slotted flaps came down 40 degrees, and at full flaps the ailerons drooped 15.5 degrees while retaining full deflection. This increase in wing camber lowered stall speed to 55 miles per hour and generated high lift for excellent climb performance. In low visibility, the typical Norseman pilot trying to figure out where he was going could cruise around and twist and turn comfortably at 65 miles per hour as long as there was gas in the tanks.

When speed was of the essence, the Norseman could attain a top speed of 160 miles per hour on wheels and 145 miles per hour on floats. With 150 imperial gallons on board, it had a range of 870 miles on wheels and 780 miles on skis or floats, and it delivered the required load-bearing ability. According to the manual, it could hoist more than 1,800 pounds of cargo, but pilots anonymously will admit to loads over 2,000 pounds, about 70 percent more than the closest rival of the day with the same engine and fuel load.

Noorduyn took an interesting approach to achieving the airplane's performance. He designed it to meet expectations on floats because he knew that it would do better on skis and wheels. Consequently, the airplane's first flight in late 1935 was on floats. It went well, but subsequent flights proved the airplane to be slightly underpowered by its 420-horsepower Wright Whirlwind engine. For the main production model, the Mark IV, which first flew in late 1936, the engine was upgraded to the 550- to 600-horsepower Pratt & Whitney Wasp. This cured the problem.

External loads are still strapped to bush planes, such as the rafters for a fishing lodge attached to this Alaskan Beaver.

The Norseman was enthusiastically embraced. More than 30 were snapped up by civilian operators in the first three years, an impressive number considering that all of Alaska had only about 175 airplanes in the late 1930s. As rumors of war from across the Atlantic turned into harsh reality, Noorduyn received the first trickle of orders for the Norseman from the allied military that soon turned into a flood.

By the eve of World War II, bush flying had become a way of life. Bush fliers had made it possible to venture into the wilderness on a scale and pace that would have been inconceivable less than a generation before. The airplane also gradually chipped away at the isolation of the scattered communities and the lone inhabitants of some of the world's remotest lands. It irrevocably changed their

A Fokker Super Universal is being loaded with cargo for a winter trip into the wilderness. Note the snowshoes, various stoves, and what appears to be prospecting tools.

Freshly caught fish have been flown to the Second Street dock in Kenika, Ontario, in a Fokker Universal. This type of fish ferrying is different from Grant McConachie's winter fish flights on skis with his Fokker.

A Canadian Stinson Jr. is still as bright and appealing as it was in the 1930s.

lives, much for the better according to most of them. The pilots flying the bush routes saw improvements in the airplanes they flew and a rudimentary system of airfields and communications slowly developed, but mostly they were still winging it on their own and relied on their skills and judgment in a world where they could afford few mistakes. And that is how most of them liked it, but the war was about to change their world as profoundly as they were changing the bush.

The Bellanca Aircruiser had unique aerodynamic wing struts that were lifting bodies. The Aircruiser is a light, strong, high-lift aircraft and was considered to be a better airplane than the Pacemaker. This one is seen at Remi Lake.

The arrival of the periodic bushplane is a major occasion in isolated villages.

Three Canadian Forest Biology Rangers load cargo into a Stinson SR-9 at the OPAS Dock Base in Temagami, Ontario. The Stinsons were OPAS' first modern cabin class aircraft and were in service into the 1950s.

A Junkers 34 falls through the ice at Chigoyan in the Northwest Territory. Such events were not uncommon in the spring when rotten ice patches were hard to identify. Leverage is being exercised with the poles to try and lift the fuselage back on solid ice. The low wing's advantage this situation was that it held most of the fuselage above water.

71

Bushplanes were valued for their ability to carry a large and bulky load. External loads have included some strange items, including entire airframe sections and an upright grand piano. Here a more conventional but bulky cargo is carried by a Canadian Junkers 34 warming up for departure at Sioux Lookout in 1934.

Not to be outdone, this Gullwing Stinson rescues the salvaged fuselage of a crashed Gypsy Moth from White Otter Lake.

The old and the new are nose to tail at Sioux Lookout in 1937. A Fairchild 71 is in front, and behind it is a brand new Norseman.

The Norseman quickly won approval from pilots and customers and markedly increased the productivity of bush flying with its greater capabilities than most aircraft used in the bush at the time. It evoked sufficient nostalgia that was commemorated in this painting by R W Bradford.

Chapter 3

The war brought larger transport and cargo aircraft to Alaska, including the C-46 Curtiss Commando, which could haul a larger load than a C-47, the military version of the DC-3, but had less-desirable flying characteristics. It can still be found sporadically in Alaskan cargo service.

War Changes Everything

On a late November day in 1938, Jack Jefford was on his routine mail run for Mirow Air Service out of Nome, Alaska, to the surrounding communities and mines. He had just left Golovin, a native village about 70 miles north of Nome, and leveled out his Gullwing Stinson at 3,500 feet, as high as the leaden overcast allowed him to climb. He was on course to cross the Darby Mountains, a low line of ridges that were more like hills, especially by Alaskan standards. But in Alaska even the hills need to be treated with great respect as the energetic young pilot who slightly resembled the swashbuckling actor Errol Flynn was about to find out.

Strong turbulence buffeted Jefford's airplane as he approached the ridge that was blanketed in 200 feet of blowing, powdery snow, but it was nothing out of the ordinary. He had a healthy altitude margin and could see well beyond the ridge line, so he pressed on. Then, without warning, the bottom fell out of the sky. Jefford had the sensation of freefalling toward the ground. He had encountered the lee of a mountain wave, and by the time he realized he should turn back, it was too late. The snow engulfed him, rocks flashed by, his world turned white, and after some chaotic confusion, he realized that although the airplane was still running at full power, it wasn't going anywhere. He shut down the howling engine and took stock. Jack Jefford crashed into a cocoon of snow without a scratch to himself and minimal damage to his airplane.

In spite of surviving the crash in such good shape he was still in deep trouble, but perhaps not as deep as he would have been even a month before. Mirow Air Service had installed its first radio in the Stinson. It transmitted in Morse code instead of voice transmission, but Jefford knew how to use it. Normally he wouldn't have been expected to be proficient in such a short time, but he had applied for a job with Pacific Alaska Airlines, the Pan American subsidiary, which required new hires to be able to transmit 13 words a minute, and he had taken it upon himself to meet the requirement.

Jefford anxiously cranked up his transmitter and carefully tapped out his distress message to Mirow Air Service several times, but there was only silence in return. Discouraged, he decided to conserve the battery, settled into his down-filled sleeping bag, and waited until about 9:00 p.m. to transmit again. This time he was thrilled to get a response from a Pacific Alaska Airlines radio operator more than 200 miles away. He managed to pass on the details of his mishap and the search was on. It still took six days for an airplane to spot him and lead a dog team to the crash site, but if he hadn't had the radio, he might have perished from a shortage of food and exposure by the time anybody could have found him.

High-tech electronics may have been decisive in saving Jefford's life, but technology wasn't the only influence trickling up into the bush from down south as his experience proved upon his return from his encounter with the Darby Mountains. Following a major reorganization in 1938, the U.S. Civil Aviation Authority's (CAA) long bureaucratic arm reached up into Alaska with a vengeance and Jefford had to fill out an accident report he thought was practically an inquisition. He got a kick out of the final question, which asked the pilot to rate his general flying ability. A great raconteur, Jefford liked to recall the answer his colleague and friend Sass Sasseen gave to that question after three crashes in quick succession: "I used to think I was pretty good, but lately I've begun to wonder."

Watson Lake Airport in the Yukon was one of many military airfields that sprung up throughout northern Canada and Alaska during World War II. This was one of several airports along Canada's Northwest Staging Route that were connected by IFR airways and formed part of the air bridge between Great Falls, Montana, and Fairbanks, Alaska. They were an important line of defense and were used to ferry lend-lease military aircraft to the Soviet Union.

Wooden-winged Cessna T-50s were among the Civil Aviation Authority's Alaska Region fleet of aircraft. They didn't stand up well to the region's harsh conditions, but thousands were built for advanced military training and nicknamed the Bamboo Bomber and Bobcat.

As aviation opened up remote areas to the outside world, it was inevitable that governments in distant capitals would assert increasing regulatory control over the freewheeling ways of the bush pilots. Although a CAA inspector had been permanently stationed in Alaska since 1934, the years of big change for Alaskan fliers were 1938 and 1939, when the Civil Aviation Authority brought to the Territory the same regulatory structure it had put in place in the rest of the United States to control what it viewed as destructive competition.

As the CAA saw it, the romantic lure of aviation had encouraged too many operators to emerge and chase a pool of passengers that was too small to sustain them all. The cutthroat pursuit to wrest business from the competition left most operators undercapitalized and struggling to survive. The financial incentive to cut corners and complete trips at all cost also potentially endangered the lives of passengers whose interests the CAA had to protect. The government's solution to this state of affairs was twofold. It established a rigorous set of technical and safety requirements under the auspices of the CAA that all air services had to be licensed and tightened the certification standards for professional pilots. It also created the Civil Aviation Board, an independent panel charged with implementing and running a system of route allocations and price controls to manage air service capacity at a level that allowed the authorized operators to make a reasonable profit.

Many of the individualistic bush pilots felt that the era of true bush flying had come to an end with the CAA's assertion of authority. But the more business minded of them welcomed the chance to operate under a more stable and predictable structure. They saw it as a better chance to stay solvent and grow as they expanded the aviation infrastructure into its next stage of development. The CAB's route allocation system remained in place for the next 40 years.

Still, there were glitches triggered by the new bureaucracy that penalized some of the experienced, responsible pilots during the transition period. The Civil Aviation Board held exhaustive hearings to determine which operators would be awarded what route rights. If existing operators

A twin-engine Sikorsky amphibian is flying the Juneau-Seattle scheduled route in 1940 when Europe was already at war. The rapid development of land airports made flying boats and amphibians obsolete, except in narrow niche uses.

Jack Jefford and colleagues deliver a stove to thaw the ground for the wartime construction of airfields throughout Alaska.

Cold Starts and Other Tricks

In their harsh operating environment, bush pilots have had to resort to a whole range of special procedures over the years to enable their airplanes to function normally. Starting an engine in ultra-cold weather is a major challenge. In the earliest days, pilots learned to drain the oil and take it inside to keep it warm. The oil would be heated before it was poured back into the engine and the pilots would place a tent around the nose of the airplane and light portable fire pots or blowtorches under the engine to heat it before starting. It was a race to start the engine before the oil congealed again and the whole process, which could take hours, would have to be repeated. Scores of aircraft burned to a crisp because of fire pot misadventures.

In the late 1920s a Canadian mechanic invented the diluter, which squirts a generous shot of gasoline into the engine oil just before shut down. The gasoline dilutes the oil so that the engine can be easily turned over. When the engine starts, the gasoline quickly burns out of the oil. The oil can be left in the crankcase, but the engine still needs to be preheated for a short time before starting.

Today there are electric heaters for the crankcases of some engines that can be plugged into any electrical outlet. Various heaters blow hot air to preheat engines, which remains a cold-weather art.

Some days it is just too cold to fly. If the temperature is below 50 degrees below zero Fahrenheit, regulations forbid flying.

Frost is an issue and is best kept off the wings of parked aircraft with tight-fitting cloth wing covers. Skis will freeze to the ground when an airplane is parked. Rocking the airplane back and forth with bursts of power usually frees them, but a better technique is to carry a block of wood to wedge under each ski to keep most of it off the ground.

Conducting repairs in the cold is also a rough task. A quick emergency field repair used by the early bush pilots for small fabric tears in weather when water instantly freezes is to smooth out the tear and slosh water over it. The water will freeze in place and join the tear. All the pilot has to do is make sure the temperature remains below zero all the way home.

Canvas nose covers channel the warmth of a fire pot within to preheat the engine. Many bushplanes were inadvertently set on fire this way.

Some other nonweather tricks are very useful to bush pilots. In a land of few refueling stops, pilots have been stashing personal gasoline supplies in the wilderness at strategic spots from the earliest days. They usually try to keep these stashes secret and hidden, as moral standards in the bush regarding unattended property are not always as high as they could be.

Oversized low-pressure tundra tires that spread an airplane's weight over a wide surface are indispensable when operating on ground that is especially soft during the spring thaw.

If a lake is not long enough for takeoff in a straight line, floatplane pilots will accelerate their aircraft in a circle on the water until it attains flying speed for take off.

Wing covers on a Canadian Fokker Universal protect it from snow and ice on the ground.

Mirow Air Service's Lockheed Vega was based in Nome, Alaska, in 1938. One of Mirow's pilots was Jack Jefford who had a narrow escape in the company's Gullwing Stinson and played a major role in establishing Alaska's airway and airport system during World War II.

could demonstrate they provided essential and continuous service on the routes they applied, the CAB would award them the routes and "grandfather" them into the new regulatory system. The benchmark period the CAB used to evaluate grandfather rights was the summer of 1938. Two of Alaska's best bush pilots, Frank Barr and Bob Reeve, had their requests rejected because they failed to meet the requirements of the grandfather clause. Neither was fully active during the period under review. Barr had made another emergency landing deep in the wilderness that kept him out of action for over a month, and a string of bad luck forced Reeve to temporarily shut his business. The two pilots weren't the only ones to think it was absurd for the bureaucrats to ignore the larger record of their experience. The CAB took until early 1942 to make its final decisions, when it awarded 22 route certificates to 21 operators.

An Experienced Young Flier Joins the CAA

The implementation of greater oversight of Alaskan aviation and plans to bring airway and airport modernization to the Territory were positive steps that would benefit aviators and passengers alike. The problem was not that change was coming to Alaskan aviation, but that it might be unduly influenced by outsiders who knew little about Alaska. One bush pilot who decided to do something about this risk was Jack Jefford. He had been waiting for an opportunity to join Pacific Alaska Airways, but he had also applied for a pilot position with the CAA and vowed to take the first job to come through. The CAA beat the PAA and Jefford accepted. In April 1940 he joined the CAA and spent the next three decades with the agency.

Jefford's timing was impeccable because the CAA was gearing up to develop Alaska's airway infrastructure, and he had a front row seat. One of his most important duties was to prove the

Galena Airfield, halfway between Anchorage and Nome, received a 5,000-foot refueling strip during the war. It flooded during the spring and was indicative of the tough seasonal conditions in the region, but the pressing need for it justified its limitations.

"Remember Dutch Harbor" never became a World War II slogan because most Alaskans would rather forget the only Japanese bombing of a large U.S. mainland settlement, which wasn't far by air from Anchorage.

new radio ranges and flight check them on a periodic schedule to maintain their accuracy. Other responsibilities included routine air support for the CAA's growing network of stations, which wasn't much different from the bush flying he had been doing before. His duties included hauling people, provisions and other supplies, equipment, mail, and building materials, and performing all the other chores of the typical bush pilot.

Jefford wasn't the only bush flier to step up to the plate for the CAA. He was joined by several equally experienced colleagues eager to bring their expertise to the agency and benefit from the steady job opportunity.

Pacific Alaska Airlines developed a basic system of radio ranges along its routes with technical help from its deep-pocketed and technology-savvy parent, Pan American Airlines, but Alaska's first public commercial radio ranges were established between July and October 1940 in Anchorage, Fairbanks, and Nome. Other ranges followed in quick succession over the coming years and increased to 56 by 1945 and spread a spider web of airways across the Territory. They transmitted low-frequency radio beams along the airways that aircraft could track en route. The system also included strategically placed fan markers around the airports, which were used in conjunction with the beams to make instrument approaches. Instrument flying had come to the bush.

A Curtiss Kingfisher prepares to leave on patrol from Attu in the Aleutians during World War II. Bob Ellis was one of several bush pilots who flew Kingfishers during the war.

In spite of the doubts expressed about such progress by many skeptical, seasoned bush pilots, there was still plenty of scope left for flying by the seat of their pants. The radio ranges were primitive devices by later standards. Each transmitter emitted four crossed beams that could be tracked by listening to the different Morse signals it emitted in each quadrant to stay centered on the beam. A cone of silence over the station indicated station passage. This was useful in tracking a specific airway, but the great majority of the scattered settlements and mines served by the bush pilots were off the airways. The ranges were excellent to establish all weather links between the major hubs and provide instrument approaches at them, but they were of little help at the typical bush strip, lake, or sandbar. Automatic direction finders that pointed at the tuned station made it possible to track specific bearings and considerably expand the utility of radio navigation, but the equipment was expensive, relatively bulky, and cantankerous. The bush pilots who liked to fly the old-fashioned way may have seen their world shrink a little with the arrival of the airways, but their preferred way of life was safe for years to come.

The Threat of War

The CAA's Alaskan airways and airport programs progressed on schedule when they received a boost from the increasingly ominous threat of war. Hundreds of millions of dollars were poured into the development of the aviation infrastructure throughout the North American wilderness during World War II in the interest of national security, as key locations within the area, especially Alaska, assumed prime strategic and tactical importance.

It is often said that America wasn't prepared for World War II, and in many respects this is true. In spite of severe isolationist pressures, however, some steps were taken to gear up the nation for war well before the Japanese attack on Pearl Harbor. One of these steps was the Development of Landing Areas for National Defense (DLAND), a massive government program to upgrade airports and construct air bases throughout the country. DLAND was initiated in 1939 and approved by Congress and launched in 1940. It eventually spent $500 million on airport infrastructure throughout the United States, and Alaska received a considerable share of it.

In spite of the general lack of military preparedness, Alaska, with its close proximity to Asia, was seen as a first line of defense by military strategists. It was also in urgent need of being equipped to meet this role. The underfunded military's presence in the region was minimal. When the Territory's commanding general wanted to tour his domain by air, he had to charter a bushplane like everyone else or commandeer one of the CAA's aircraft.

The main problem with building and maintaining a military presence in Alaska to adequately meet the perceived strategic objectives was access. In the absence of a road or rail link with the lower 48 states, the only effective way to ship large quantities of men and materiel to the Territory was by sea, a slow, time-consuming, and sometimes seasonal process.

In spite of the advances of aviation within Alaska, there was still no reliable air link to the outside world, which was crucial for the rapid movement of key personnel and vital supplies and for positioning air power even before the creation of Air Transport Command and its massive airlift capability that would emerge during the coming war. The coastal route, plagued by atrocious weather and without an IFR airway system, was considered marginally reliable and impractical.

To meet America's sudden need for a dependable air link to Alaska, an inland route would have to be developed where the weather was more manageable and airports and airways could be easily established and developed. But that raised the need for cooperation from Canada. Fortunately for the United States, the Canadian government was in some respects even further ahead than its southern neighbor in its commitment to develop its airway and airport infrastructure in the country's western wilderness areas along the inland route between Alaska and the lower 48 states of the United States.

Bob Reeve's Boeing 80 is loaded with a heavy boiler during the construction of Northway Airport, halfway between Whitehorse and Fairbanks. Reeve and others flew in 1,100 tons of supplies in five months to construct the most remote airport on the Northwest Staging Route.

A Noorduyn Norseman in U.S. Army Air Force service taxies out for an early-morning support flight. The Norseman, the only purpose-built bushplane in the 1940s, filled an important role as a military liaison aircraft and was used by armed forces on several continents.

The U.S. military bought more than 700 Norsemen and designated them UC 64. They were used in large numbers to support the Alaska Highway and the Northwest Staging Route.

An early model U.S. Army Air Corps Beech 18 was used primarily for aerial mapping. Thousands of Beech 18s were built for the military, and many became bushplanes after the war.

Canada shared America's concerns with its western defenses, but its commitment to develop aviation in its western territories were civilian in origin and preceded concerns about defense. In 1938 the Canadian government gave civil aviation a major boost by forming Trans Canada Airlines, the national flag carrier that became Air Canada and had a monopoly on scheduled transcontinental and mainline services.

This was not exactly welcome news to the country's entrepreneurial band of ultracompetitive bush operators. They saw their own opportunities grow into scheduled airlines quashed by government decree. But the government saw too much competition as a serious hindrance to the stable development of scheduled air service and opted for the national flag carrier solution.

Concurrently the government initiated the development of the infrastructure that its new airline would need to operate nationwide. It included several strategically placed civilian airports in the west and northwest with an eye to eventually establishing a trans-Pacific air route via Alaska. The possibility of a trans-Pacific route through Northwestern Canada had long excited Pan American's Juan Trippe and the more visionary members of the Canadian aviation community, particularly Grant McConachie. There was also government interest. As early as 1935, officials of Canada's Department of Transport hired Punch Dickins to fly them on an epic 8,400-mile survey flight to scout routes and potential airport locations for the air link to the Orient.

As Canada was compelled to enter World War II as a member of the British Commonwealth, long before Pearl Harbor, the plans for its western and northwestern airports assumed a new importance and urgency. They were a crucial component of Canada's defenses against any threat from the Pacific. The Canadian government launched a crash program to develop a reliable, permanent military/civilian air link between Edmonton and Whitehorse, which was called the Northwest Staging Route.

Ironically, Canadian Airways' German Junkers fleet flew throughout the Canadian bush during the war. Here the company's unusual single-engine Junkers 52 is parked next to a Lockheed Electra at Red Lake, Ontario.

The Lockheed Lodestar was a good, smaller alternative to the DC-3. It was faster and benefited from the same advanced aviation technology. It was a mainstay of the Pan American fleet that served Alaska. Pan Am turned its subsidiary, Pacific Alaska Airways, into a division and expanded aggressively in Alaska during the war.

Five airports were designated to be built or substantially upgraded from primitive strips in this phase of the program. The airports were in Grande Prairie, Alberta; Fort Saint John and Fort Nelson in British Columbia; and Watson Lake and Whitehorse in the Yukon. The route was pioneered by bush pilots, particularly Grant McConachie's struggling, cheerful airline that had carried the mail to Whitehorse since 1937. It was now named Yukon Southern Air Transport. As McConachie dreamed of service all the way to Shanghai while he trundled up to Whitehorse in his rattling Ford Trimotor, his airline was hard at work to develop short, rudimentary landing strips along the route, which formed the basis of the government's Northwest Staging Route.

In mid-1940 Canada and the United States formed a Permanent Joint Board of Defense to address mutual concerns about the war and coordinate threat responses. It was a logical step for the board to extend the Northwest Staging Route from Edmonton down to the United States in the south and from Whitehorse to Fairbanks in the north to establish America's air bridge to Alaska. In addition to rebuilding already existing fields in the United States and Fairbanks, other primary airfields added to the route were at Dawson Creek, British Columbia, where there was a railhead, and Northway, Alaska. By September 1941, the route was open for business under visual flight rules, and by December, its radio beam network was completed and open to IFR traffic.

Several factors, including the attack by Germany on the Soviet Union in June 1941, hastened the creation of the Northwest Staging Route soon after the original plans for the air bridge were launched. In spite of America's wariness of entering World War II prior to Pearl Harbor, the U.S. Congress had approved a lend-lease program in March 1941 to aid any country fighting the Axis powers. The intention was primarily to aid Britain with military equipment, but when the Soviet Union was attacked, the Roosevelt Administration immediately envisioned a substantial lend-lease

Anything, Anytime, Anywhere

The pilot of the Pilatus Porter was especially grateful for his airplane's short field performance as he stalled it onto the jungle strip's threshold in the morning haze and braked hard to stop in 200 feet. A stream of tracers coming straight at him confirmed his suspicion that the enemy still held the strip's other end. He was dropping off a hot load, his company's code for the ammunition on board, to help retake the field. His next trip would be a cold load, a rice drop to a friendly hamlet.

The jungle strip was deep in the mountains of Laos, and the pilot flew for Air America, the U.S. Central Intelligence Agency's secret air service operated by civilian contract pilots, in a secret war next door to Vietnam during the 1960s. The Cold War's two major protagonists were determined to pretend that their standoff wasn't boiling over in this officially neutral backwater, where they supported opposing sides of a divided population that was fighting it out in the hills. When Air America's ragtag bushplanes based at Vientiane Airport were done ferrying supplies and passengers all over the jungle, they parked next to the Soviet transports that brought ammo and equipment from the East Block for the guys who took potshots at them all day. The senior U.S. official in Laos who was ultimately responsible for the unusual U.S. air service attended the same diplomatic cocktail parties as his Soviet counterparts and their local protégés.

Air America favored the expensive Swiss Pilatus Porters, which had excellent STOL capability.

Air America's motto was "Anything, anytime, anywhere," and its bush operations were classic bush flying with a twist. There were no air regulations to worry about; a lot of unmapped terrain to fly over; the roughest, shortest, most uneven strips imaginable; no navigational aids; some of the world's foulest, rainiest weather; and you were shot at, to boot. No Geneva Convention applied to your civilian rear end if you crashed and the wrong guys rescued you. But the pilots were there for more than the authentic bush flying and the combat zone thrills. In a few months they could earn what it would take them a decade to make if they were transporting tourists in the North American Wilderness.

program for the Soviets as well, including the supply of combat and transport aircraft. The aircraft were delivered to the beleaguered Soviet Union along the excruciatingly long, but secure airway up the Northwest Staging Route into Alaska, across to Siberia, and on to the Soviet frontlines through the back door, which was the only practical route thanks to the frontlines in Europe.

The Alaska Highway

After the attack on Pearl Harbor, lend-lease efforts to the Soviet Union were accelerated as the United States expanded its effort to link Alaska and the rest of the United States to face the very real threat from Japan. The first step was the immediate approval of the Alaska Highway. Various routes had been under consideration for some time, but the war's urgency brought the decision to lay out the road to track the Northwest Staging Route. The highway's primary purpose was to support the air bridge and act as a navigation aid to the inexperienced crews.

The need for additional, secondary airfields was also addressed. They were needed as emergency fields and to support the highway's construction. A good example of this support was Dawson Creek where the rail lines ended and the Alaska Highway officially began. Other secondary fields were the Sikanni Chief, Prophet, Beatton, Liard, and Smith rivers in British Columbia; Pine Lake, Squanga Lake, Pon Lake, Teslin, Haines Junction, Aishihik, Burwash, and Snag in Yukon Territory; and Tanacross in Alaska. By the time the last of the secondary fields was completed in 1944, the longest stretch between airports along the air bridge was a mere 140 miles. Many of these airports are still active today.

An early beneficiary of these war plans was Canadian bushplane manufacturer Noorduyn Norseman Aircraft Ltd. The company's order book approached 100 prewar, an impressive number for its time that was dwarfed by the orders that flooded in after the war broke loose. The U.S. Army Air Force (USAAF) and the Royal Canadian Air Force (RCAF) signed up for Norsemen by the hundreds. The United States initially used them to support the construction and management of the air bridge to Alaska and the Alaska Highway. They were also used by both armed forces for general training, utility, and ambulance purposes. Designated the UC-64 by the USAAF, the Norseman's military version was a Mark IV that was modified to include the military gear specified by the buyers. A total of 767 Norsemen were purchased by the military during World War II. By 1943 Noorduyn employed more than 11,000 people to build them, which was up from 130 in early 1940 (this workforce produced

> *"I'd rather fly in Alaska and live on beans than fly down here [in Portland, Oregon] and own a Rolls Royce."*
>
> —Russell Merrill

The fur flying attire, which was the only way to keep warm in the north's extreme cold, slowly gave way to synthetic arctic clothing developed during the war.

A C-47, the military version of the DC-3, flies over the volcanic Aleutian chain of islands.

other aircraft types for the military alongside the Norseman). In addition to the North American bush, Norsemen also served in Europe, Asia, South America, and the South Pacific.

As the inland air and road links to Alaska began to take shape, the construction of DLAND airfields and airbases progressed throughout the Territory. Ladd Field in Fairbanks became the main terminus of the air bridge and the pickup point for Russian crews of the lend-lease aircraft destined for the Soviet Union. It was supported by nearby Mile 26 Field, which was renamed Eileson Air Base. Nome became a major air base and was the last U.S. port of call on the way to Siberia. Galena, about halfway between Fairbanks and Nome, received a 5,000-foot airstrip to serve as a refueling base. In Anchorage, Elmendorf Air Field became the region's principal air base. Cordova, Gulkana, Big Delta, Barrow, Bethel, McGrath, King Salmon, and in the Southeast Yakutat, Gustavus, Annette Island just south of Ketchikan, and Juneau were among the many sites that received the DLAND treatment.

While the CAA managed most of the airfield construction on the Alaskan mainland, the military built a string of air bases along the 1,500-mile-long chain of the Aleutian Islands. America's worst fears were realized when the Japanese bombed Dutch Harbor on Unalaska Island in the summer of 1942. It wasn't far from the western tip of the mainland and then the Japanese occupied Attu and Kiska, two of the islands farthest west in the Aleutian chain. This was the only instance in modern times that a foreign power occupied U.S. soil. Although it came a few weeks after the U.S. victory in the Battle of Midway that broke the back of Japan's carrier force, it was kept fairly quiet in the wartime media and threw the military establishment into a high state of anxiety and indignation. It didn't amuse the Alaskans either. It took a year to gear up for the counterattack, and when it came it claimed more U.S. lives than both Gulf Wars combined.

The lend-lease aircraft deliveries to the Soviet Union commenced in earnest along the air bridge from the lower 48 states at about the same time the Japanese gained their foothold in the Aleutians. Its southern staging point was Great Falls, Montana. From there pilots of the USAAF's 7th Ferry Group flew the aircraft up to Fairbanks where the Soviets accepted them for the long trans-Siberian flight to the frontlines. After a slow start, the stream of aircraft became a flood. By the end of the war, 7,926 aircraft had been delivered via the air bridge to the Soviet Air Force. More than 5,000 were fighters, mostly P-39 Airacobras and P-40s; about 2,000 were A-20 and B-25 bombers; and 710 were C-47 transports, the military version of the DC-3. The stream of aircraft heading for the Soviet Union was dubbed the Red Star Line. The white stars they wore to Fairbanks were painted red before they were handed over to the Russians.

B-25 Mitchell medium bombers at Ladd Field in Fairbanks are prepared for a frigid flight. Of the 7,926 aircraft ferried to the Soviet Union along the air bridge to Siberia, more than 1,000 were B-25s. U.S. pilots flew them to Fairbanks where the white stars were painted red and the Russian pilots took over and continued on through Nome.

Meanwhile, as Air Transport Command's capabilities grew exponentially during the war, a flood of DC-3s, C-46 Curtiss Commandos, and the new four-engine C-54s (the military version of the DC-4) trooped back and forth between Alaska and the lower 48. The flights were operated mainly on contract by Pan American, Northwest, United, and Western airlines. Northwest seized the opportunity to transform itself from a small, regional carrier into a national airline. The trademark bright red tails of Northwest's airliners originated from this period. They were painted red to help aerial search-and-rescue parties spot them if they were forced down.

The inland air bridge to Alaska worked very well, but the lure of an airway along the shorter coastal route continued to appeal, especially to West Coast operators. In 1942, the CAA's Alaska Division and its pilot Jack Jefford pushed one through. By then, Alaskan airway segments went as far south as Annette Island near Ketchikan, and the airway from the south extended slightly to the north of Vancouver, British Columbia. Three additional coastal radio ranges bridged the gap and the long coveted coastal (IFR) Instrument Flight Rules link between the south and Alaska became a reality.

One factor that made the route more reliable and manageable than originally envisioned was the discovery by Jefford and his colleagues that the weather was considerably more benign offshore than alongside the massive Coastal Mountains laced with peaks towering as high as 19,000 feet. While the fog and rain were every bit as bad and prolific as expected, some distance offshore the mess could be routinely topped by about 7,000 to 8,000 feet for a smooth, clear ride. They laid out segments of the airways accordingly, as geography permitted, and IFR flights along the coastal route became just another fact of life in the system of airways that involved the entire globe in the interest of war.

A windfall of World War II was the inexpensive surplus availability of airplanes, such as the Noorduyn Norseman, suited for bush flying. This Interior Airways' Norseman is shown here in a later conflict with the Distant Early Warning radar line in the 1950s to warn of approaching Soviet bombers.

Military Contracts and Predictable Pay

The wider world of aviation swept into the bush during the war like a summer storm. Business evaporated as civilian flying came to a practical standstill, but when the military geared up to a full wartime footing, bush pilots found themselves better off than they ever were before. Bush flying became an indispensable transportation link in the implementation of the massive projects brought by the war. The armed forces, government agencies, and civilian contractors all vied for the services of the bush pilots to get them to the inaccessible places where they had to perform construction miracles on tight deadlines. The pilots also kept personnel and supplies flowing while they got their jobs done. The contracts they gave the bush pilots were sound and often long term, and the government and the contractors it employed were good risk. The paperwork could have been a bit less, but the bush operators made more money on a more predictable basis than they ever had.

The most upsetting setback experienced bush fliers faced was that they were turned down when they volunteered for combat flying assignments in the major theaters of war. Some were over the age limit, but many of the younger experienced pilots were also turned down. While their less experienced colleagues were shipped out to fly worldwide for Uncle Sam or the Queen, they were deemed to have highly desirable specialist skills, namely they really knew how to fly the bush, so that's where they stayed. Jack Jefford was told that his services to the CAA to shepherd the completion of the massive airway and airport infrastructure expansion work in the Territory was more important than flying a bomber or a fighter on the other side of the world.

Even when an experienced bush pilot was taken into the armed forces, he was more likely to be assigned to military flying in his area of expertise than in another theater. Bob Ellis of Ellis Airways, a U.S. Naval Academy graduate and Naval reserve officer, was called up immediately after Pearl Harbor and was promptly instructed to return to Sitka and fly one of his own Waco floatplanes on antisubmarine patrol in the first surreal days of the war. He put a Springfield rifle onboard for close

Floats of Fancy

A plane's floats are rarely made by the aircraft's manufacturer. For most aircraft that can fly on floats, they are an option and aircraft manufacturers hand off the task to specialist firms. Making floats has a lot in common with boat building. The float manufacturers can realize economies of scale and design floats that can be used on a variety of aircraft.

One of the oldest and most venerable names in floats is EDO. The company was founded in 1925 by Earl Dodge Osborne (whose initials form the name of the company) on Long Island, which was a hotbed of aircraft design at the time. Osborne aspired to be an airplane builder, and EDO's first product was a seaplane. Seaplanes were such a large segment of the market that he realized he could corner a niche by becoming the premiere float producer.

EDO's floats were soon on scores of designs, including Charles and Anne Lindbergh's Lockheed Sirius that took them on 29,000 miles of survey flights for Pan American all over the world in 1933.

Above: Manufacture and overhaul of MacDonald-Edo Seaplane Floats. Edo floats and float spare parts are available for other makes of aircraft, including Otter, Beaver, Norseman, Piper, Aeronca, etc.

HERE IT IS!
A NEW HIGH-BUOYANCY EDO FLOAT FOR CESSNA 180

Completely new in design and available now

The latest Edo Model 2870 Floats provide increased buoyancy for the Cessna 180 float plane with improved performance and water maneuverability. Displacement, 2,870 lbs. Complete installation weight, 378 lbs.

New MacDonald-built 2870 Floats are available for early delivery on orders placed now. Contact your nearest Cessna dealer for further details or write MacDonald Bros. Aircraft Ltd.

Edo FLOATS

CESSNA AIRCRAFT DEALERS
QUEBEC
MONTREAL—Laurentide Aviation Ltd.
ONTARIO
MALTON—Sanderson Aircraft, Ltd.
MANITOBA
BRANDON—Brandon Air Services, Ltd.
SASKATCHEWAN
MELFORT—Reliable Air Service
REGINA—Prairie Flying Service
ALBERTA
CALGARY—Foothills Aviation, Ltd.
BRITISH COLUMBIA
VANCOUVER—Vancouver's U-Fly

MACDONALD BROS. AIRCRAFT LIMITED
WINNIPEG - OTTAWA - VANCOUVER

For decades the EDO corporation was the prime floatplane pontoon builder.

EDO scrambled to find alternatives to the drastically declining demand for seaplanes after World War II and built a successful diversified defense and aerospace company. It continued to meet the needs of the civilian floatplane market and it continued to be the premiere float maker in the world for decades. The amphibious float with retractable wheels was developed around that time and was an interesting alternative to regular floats.

Eventually the float business no longer fit into the company's core activities and today Kenmore Air of Seattle, Washington, builds and supports floats and holds the rights to EDO floats. Other successful float makers in this skilled niche market include Wipline, the largest float manufacturer today with the broadest product range; Aerocet, which specializes in composite floats; Baumann; and Aqua.

Floatplane pontoons are more of a nautical art than aeronautics.

Bushplanes, such as this Gullwing Stinson, were used prominently to support wartime activities. Many bush pilots were not accepted for military service because their special expertise was needed in the bush.

combat, installed a door in the floor through which he could toss out bombs, and went off to hunt for Japanese subs in the company Waco. As the military machine trundled into high gear, a Kingfisher floatplane scouting squadron materialized at Sitka, and Ellis became its executive officer and then its commander. The squadron ended up in the Aleutians where Ellis ultimately became the commanding officer of Naval Air Station Attu after it was retaken from the Japanese.

One of the best examples of how civilian bush pilots thrived while giving indispensable wartime service to their country is Bob Reeve. Through a run of bad luck, he had been without his own airplanes and temporarily out of business just before the war broke out. He was able to keep working through the kindness of his good friend Noel Wien who was willing to help him out until he regained his footing. The break that put him back in his own cockpit was the war.

One of the most challenging airports to build on the Northwest Staging Route was the airport at Northway, halfway between Whitehorse and Fairbanks. It could be approached by river from Tetlin, but it would have required months of organization and transport to get the required equipment and supplies for the construction of the airport to the site. The project didn't have that kind of time. Morrison-Knudsen Company, the construction company that was contracted to build Northway looked hard for the right bush pilot to help out and found Bob Reeve.

Reeve flew Morrison-Knudsen's foreman to Tetlin and the two took a boat to the site with a skeleton construction crew. In six days they hacked out a strip long enough for Reeve's Fairchild 71. They had the equipment trucked to the closest mine with a roadhead, which was about 50 miles away. They turned part of the road at the mine into an airstrip, and Bob Reeve went to work. Within five months, the organization he organized moved 1,100 tons of equipment and supplies and 300 construction workers to the Northway site by flying seven days a week from sunup to sundown. Morrison-Knudsen bought Reeve a Boeing 80A to augment the Fairchild. Mudhole Smith of Cordova Airlines and other bush pilots whose skills were too valuable to be employed in other types of flying for the war effort joined Reeve in part of the airlift.

Reeve's big contribution to the war was yet to come. Following the Northway job, he was disappointed that the CAA wouldn't assign him any grandfathered rights to the service he built out of Valdez because he was out of action during the CAA's means testing period. So he tackled the Aleutian Island chain, the only area of Alaska to which the bush-flying community hadn't provided regular air service. The armed forces wanted charter service along the islands to its main stations, and Reeve provided it.

The Aleutians have a reputation for the foulest weather in Alaska and take the brunt of the North Pacific's monster low-pressure systems. They average more and worse fog and precipitation than southeastern Alaska, and winds commonly howl for days at speeds exceeding 100 miles per hour. Flying out of Anchorage, Reeve supplied the Aleutians throughout the war with good judgment, patience, and just enough aggressiveness to push through with sufficient reliability to effectively deliver the service the military contracted him to provide.

Bob Reeve's major contribution to the war was establishing a reliable supply service throughout the challenging 1,000-mile-long Aleutian island chain. Reeve flew a bright red Fairchild 71, like the one seen here, in Wien's service. He turned his bush venture into Reeve Aleutian Airlines after the war and upgraded to surplus DC-3s and then to flying turboprops and Boeing jets.

Jean Potter, who wrote about Alaskan bush flying in her book, *The Flying North*, accompanied Reeve on one of these flights during the war. Her account of the trip illustrates the challenges faced by Reeve, the old-fashioned bush pilot in his minimally equipped Fairchild, and how his world contrasted with the encroaching world of capable modern aircraft equipped with the latest navigation aids. The flight from Anchorage to Cold Bay, where the mainland ends and the island chain begins, started out in sunshine, but by the time the Fairchild approached its destination, the fog rolled in. Reeve stumbled along at reduced air speed and skimmed the surface until everything turned white. He then firewalled the throttle and pulled up the Fairchild's nose. They broke out at 7,000 feet into unlimited visibility above the solid cloud layer in time to see a formation of bombers tracking the airway.

The bombers peeled off at precise intervals, sank into the clouds, and were on the ground at Cold Bay in minutes following routine instrument approaches. Without a navigation receiver on board, Reeve had to resort to his wily bush pilot ways. Failing to find a hole through which he could let down, he noted his position by two volcanoes sticking out of the undercast and headed out to sea on a bearing, knowing that there were no obstructions in his way. He eased down into the murky clouds as confidently as the bombers had and kept his eyes peeled for the ocean. It soon loomed in the windshield with 200 feet to spare. Flying at only 60 miles per hour, Reeve carefully reversed course, taking great care not to lose the water surface from sight. Eventually the shoreline materialized in the misty gloom and Reeve's superbly detailed terrain knowledge allowed him to grope his way to the airport for a safe landing.

Sig Wien was another pilot whose civilian services to the military were greatly appreciated. In Barrow, his Wien Alaska Airlines base and America's northernmost settlement, he provided crucial support for the U.S. Navy's Arctic oil-drilling program, the precursor to the exploitation of the North Slope oil fields. Much of the Navy's early work on the project consisted of geological surveying, where Wien's intimate knowledge of the terrain and conditions proved invaluable. In some critical situations, he was able to land and retrieve survey teams under difficult terrain and conditions with much greater efficiency than the Navy.

Harold Gillam, the infamous bad weather flier, also signed up to fly for Morrison-Knudsen Company to support the air bases the company was constructing. Morrison-Knudsen bought him a

The de Havilland Dragon Rapide came into service in the late 1930s and was widely used in the Canadian bush in passenger and cargo service throughout the war and beyond.

sleek, new twin-engine Lockheed Electra. Gillam flew the Electra just as hard as any of his airplanes and flew all over Alaska and even south to Seattle on occasion, continuing to barge into the worst weather. Having pioneered his own brand of weather flying, he was reluctant to adhere to the CAA's standardized ways when he felt he knew better, which was often, and this led to frequent altercations with the authorities.

As good a pilot as he was, Gillam accumulated a big advance on sheer luck in his many close calls over his career. On a foul January day in 1943 on a flight from Seattle to Annette Island near Ketchikan, the time finally came to pay the bill. As one of the fiercest storms in half a century was about to bash into the coast, every flight heading north to Alaska from Seattle was canceled, except for Harold Gillam's. He was off with five passengers and barreled through the storm toward his destination and was well within range on the airways. It is said that at some point obsolete charts may have caused confusion regarding his position. According to a credible passenger who worked for the CAA, Gillam began to fly a pattern to try and orient himself in the solid instrument conditions, cruising at 6,000 feet as ice ominously built on the wings.

At this point, one of the Electra's engines quit and Gillam was in serious trouble. Most twin-engine piston airplanes don't have enough power on one engine to perform well. They can be nursed to a landing at a considerably lower altitude than they can attain on two engines, but any complicating factor, such as a heavy load or ice on the airframe, will make the pilot's life much more difficult and potentially shorter. Gillam's Electra sank ominously, rapidly shedding 4,000 feet as the increasingly concerned passengers found themselves looking up at rocks and trees in a momentary break in the fog and darkness. The Electra swerved to avoid a jagged granite outcrop and faced another one dead ahead. Gillam applied full power and aimed the airplane at just above its lowest point. He didn't make it.

The right wing hit a tree and the Electra spun around and scattered itself across the ground. As grim as the crash was, it could have been worse. Gillam and all his passengers were alive, though injured, in various degrees. There was reason to hope for rescue. After all, as Gillam knew, hundreds had been found in similar circumstances. He got to work setting up shelter, finding and stashing the emergency rations that were on board, and preparing signal fires.

The obstinate bush pilot failed to do the one thing that could have most helped him and his passengers in their predicament. He had not given a single position report on the radio all day. He had stubbornly flown the entire trip in radio silence. As he struggled with the stricken Electra, he managed to get off one brief, frantic radio call on being in trouble. It was picked up, but contained no useful information. As far as the world knew, he could have been anywhere between Seattle and Ketchikan.

A massive search was launched along the entire coast but nothing was found and the search was called off after three weeks, which was too soon to some who remembered Gillam participating in epic searches. A month after the crash, a passing boat spotted two ragged survivors who had hiked down to the shore and built a big, smoking fire in an attempt to increase the group's chances of being found. Two other survivors were barely alive at the crash site in horribly wet and cold conditions. One was dead, and Gillam, who had left them earlier to try and get a better bearing on their location, hadn't returned. The rescuers found him by the water, wrapped in his parachute, dead from exposure and injuries. They were only 16 miles from Ketchikan.

Adapting to Change

Harold Gillam wasn't alone in having difficulties adapting to change as the rugged individualist battling the elements was gradually being replaced by a more cooperative approach that brought an increasingly useful aviation infrastructure to support the pilot's job, accompanied by more rules and regulations. But the majority adjusted and willingly embraced technical advances and recognized the reasons at least for the more sensible regulations. Many bush pilots voluntarily installed two-way communications radios before 1941, when they became mandatory for aircraft-carrying passengers in Alaska. They learned to benefit from the system and reverted to rugged individualist mode only when they had the chance to fly the old-fashioned way, which still turned out to be most of the time away from the airways and the larger settlements.

The war also brought consolidation among Alaska's bush operators. In the early 1940s, several smaller air services were absorbed by Anchorage-based Star Air Lines, including Nome's Mirow Air Service, whose founder, Hans Mirow perished in a crash on a search mission in 1939. Following the acquisitions, Star changed its name to Alaska Star Airlines, and then Alaska Airlines, which it is still called today.

As World War II was drawing to its end in 1945, another consolidation took place between seven small independent operators who felt the squeeze from the bigger outfits such as Wien and Alaska Airlines. They were Petersen Air Service, Jim Dodson Air Service, Bristol Bay Air Service, Northern Airways, the remnants of Gillam Airways, Walatka Air Service, and Northern Air Service. These independent operators, which were located throughout Alaska, realized that by combining forces, they could compete with the Territory-wide services of the bigger air carriers and would have a chance for further growth. Starting with a patchwork fleet that included a Stinson Trimotor, Norsemen, Stinsons, and surplus DC-3s, Northern Consolidated Airways turned into one of Alaska's main regional carriers and flew until 1970 when it merged with Wien Alaska Airlines.

Canadian Bush Fliers

The wartime fortunes of bush fliers in Canada were initially considerably tougher than the experiences of their contemporaries in Alaska. Canada entered the war in September 1939, much earlier than the United States, and imposed severe restrictions on the civilian economy to preserve resources. This policy was not immediately accompanied by a rapid expansion of economic activity to support the war. Consequently, the demand for civilian aviation plummeted and no alternative replaced it, practically grounding the air services.

Consolidation among Alaskan bush services took place during the war. Five small companies merged to form Northern Consolidated Airways, and, Star Airlines acquired several smaller operators and became Alaska Star Airlines and then Alaska Airlines, which it is still called today.

Canadian Pacific Air Lines was formed by Canadian Pacific Railroad to rescue 10 smaller struggling bush services. It played a key support role in the Canadian bush during World War II and became a major international airline under the leadership of its charismatic president, Grant McConachie, who began his career hauling fish in a Fokker Universal.

BUILDING MORE PLANES

means building BETTER planes that cost LESS

SETTLE your family in a new Piper Cub, take to the air smoothly, and sit back for a new experience in travel. You're enjoying the benefits of fifteen years of plane-making . . . of *building more planes* than produced by all other light-plane makers combined. Consider the price of a Piper Cub—as little as $665 down—less than any other personal plane. *Building more planes* made this possible . . . Notice how this lane takes off and lands almost by itself, at a safe, easy-going speed. *Building more planes* perfected this de design . . . And when you set your Piper Cub own after that business or pleasure trip, figure your

gas mileage. Better than the average car! Economy like that isn't found on a drawing board—it's the result of *building more planes.*

See the new Piper Cubs at your dealer's now. The Super Sea Scout, illustrated, is the Super Cruiser with the additional equipment of floats—a three-passenger, 100-horsepower plane with an electric starter. The Special is a two-passenger, 65-horsepower plane—also obtainable with floats. Ask your dealer for a free flight demonstration . . . have him tell you about the convenient payment terms, and the *free flying course* included with the purchase of every new Piper Cub.

HERE ARE 3 FINE AVIATION BOOKS FOR *You!*

1. *Piper Cub Brochure.* Brand new! Beautiful, full-color airplane illustrations, suitable for framing. Complete specifications of Piper Cubs.
2. *"How to Fly" Book.* Takes you on a typical flying lesson with 35 step-by-step photos and descriptions. Many other interesting facts.
3. *"What Your Town Needs" Book.* Will help you or your community plan an inexpensive landing area now. Get these books from your Piper Cub Dealer now. Or, if you prefer, send to us for each or 25c for all three. Use stamps or coins. Specify which books you desire. Write Dept. L26.

PIPER AIRCRAFT CORPORATION
LOCK HAVEN, PENNA., U. S. A.
In Canada: Cub Aircraft Ltd., Hamilton

OOK TO THE LEADER FOR GOOD SAFE PLANES YOU CAN AFFORD TO BUY AND FLY

PIPER

As the war wound down, airplane manufacturers hoped for rapid growth in civilian private flying, which was reflected in their advertising. Piper's Cub series of aircraft found a niche in bush flying, especially when the line matured into the light, powerful Super Cub within a few years.

The monopoly trunk carrier, TCA, was kept afloat by the government, but the bush operators found themselves in a dismal economic position. They were desperate for business and their very existence was threatened. Many of the bush pilots found ways to serve in the armed forces; the younger ones as pilots with operational units, and the older ones in the vast training organization set up by the Royal Canadian Air Force to churn out military fliers for the Commonwealth. Bush operators and the pilots who remained with them wondered how long they would last in the business.

Canadian bush flying was rescued from its bleak prospects by one of the country's toughest capitalist enterprises, the Canadian Pacific Railroad (CPR). The CPR was much more than a train operator. It was one of the most diversified companies in Canada with interests ranging far beyond its core railroad business. Included in its holdings were a major shipping line, a national hotel business, mining and smelting interests, substantial real estate interests, an international telegraph business, and numerous service businesses serving its vast rail network.

The CPR had long had an interest in entering the air transportation field to complement its railroad and shipping lines and was somewhat disappointed in the government's decision to monopolize the mainline airline business. However, it had an investment in Canadian Airlines, and in the crisis faced by the bush-flying community, it saw the chance to enter the air service business in a big way at an attractive price.

Consequently, in 1941, the CPR bought Canada's top 10 bush air services and combined them into a new entity called Canadian Pacific Airlines. Among the firms purchased were Canadian Airways, McKenzie Air Service, and Yukon Southern Air Transport.

Soon after the CPR rescued bush aviation, the opportunities picked up considerably for Canada's bush pilots. The Northern Staging Route and Alaska Highway projects both required their support. As the allies geared up to go on the offensive in World War II, there was also a revival of activity in the natural resources industries. The government was willing to develop or upgrade airports and navigation aids to the remotest corners of Canada if a strategically important mine warranted it.

The war brought about an important change in the nature of Canadian bush flying. As hard-surface airports appeared throughout the bush, the role of the floatplanes slowly began to diminish in favor of wheeled aircraft. This was the beginning of a process that accelerated significantly after the war when the government embarked on a large nationwide civilian airport building program. The gradual switch to wheels was a welcome development given the modern wheeled aircraft's greater aerodynamic efficiency, which allowed higher speed and greater load-bearing capacity.

Canada's bush pilots also supported a project that wasn't as well known as the construction and operation of the Alaska Highway, but was equally arduous. The Canol Pipeline project was the construction of a 600-mile-long oil pipeline from the Norman Wells oil fields along the Mackenzie River to a refinery in Whitehorse. From here, the refined gasoline would be distributed along the upper reaches of the Alaska Highway and the region's airfields. The pipeline was built, but it had many opponents from the beginning. It led to political infighting, proved to be uneconomical, and was abandoned by the war's end. The pipeline project may have ended in failure, but the bush pilots provided sterling support for it while it lasted.

One of the more interesting developments to come out of the war for bush pilots was the emergence of several types of aircraft suitable for bush flying, chief among them the Grumman Goose and the PBY Catalina. Both aircraft were amphibians, equally at home on runways and water and both played important postwar roles.

World War II's effect on the bush-flying landscape was dramatic. In Alaska, the U.S. military, DLAND projects, and numerous other programs spent several hundred million dollars on the aviation infrastructure. More than 30 primary airports were hacked out of the bush and up to code with modern air carrier and military standards. Almost as many secondary fields were built for support and emergency use. There were 56 radio ranges installed, which provided more than 8,000 miles of modern airways throughout the Territory. The Alaska Highway cost $115 million for the United States alone. The Canadians spent an equally lavish amount for the airports along the Northwest Staging Route and on training and staging fields throughout the country. Canada also made equally important advances in the expansion of its radio navigation system.

These developments brought a dramatic increase in civilian aviation in the postwar wilderness. In many respects, flying in these areas wasn't much different from flying anywhere else. But those who foretold the end of bush flying were proven wrong.

The speedy, modern Lockheed Electra came into service in the mid-1930s and quickly became a popular feeder liner on routes too sparse for the DC-3. Harold Gillam was flying an Electra for Morrison Knudsen when he crashed near Ketchikan after an engine failure in bad weather and died.

First plane to land at the Pacific Alaska Airways Airport Juneau Alaska Mar 25, 1935

The world's favorite bushplane, the de Havilland DHC-2 Beaver, was introduced in 1947 and combined numerous performance and economic attributes into a magic formula that has yet to be replaced.

A Way of Life

Don Braun's favorite way to spend his rare summer Sundays off during the 1950s was to pile his wife and three young boys into the family's Republic SeaBee amphibian and fly out from Yellowknife to a nearby lake for a picnic. He recalls one outing to Fisherman's Lake in his memoirs, *Arctic Fox*. As they returned from a customary walk after their picnic, they were surprised to find a big black bear pawing through the remnants of their lunch.

Braun tersely instructed his family to take a detour down to the beach and pile into the SeaBee as fast as they could. He turned to distract the bear to buy the family more time to reach the airplane. His wife and sons made it safely, but Braun was in a bind. He clutched an 8-pound trout he had just caught and faced an apparently hungry bear between him and his picnic accessories and airplane. At least a large spruce tree shielded him somewhat from the bear. The decisive bush pilot quickly devised a plan. He would toss the trout to one side of the tree for the bear to go after. As the bear made off with this fish Braun would run around the tree's other side, rush for the SeaBee, snatch the family lunch box and coffee pot on the way, and beat a hasty retreat into the air.

The amazed bear watched the trout sail across the sky and land with a thud tantalizingly close by and sauntered right past it and headed straight for the tree. Braun sat tight, but the bear ambled along beyond him without as much as a sniff. Braun bolted for the SeaBee, pined for the trout, and saw the indifferent bear rambling safely off in the distance as he hit the beach.

Republic RC-3 SeaBee

Year introduced: 1946
Engine: 215-horsepower Franklin
Fuel: 75 gallons
Gross weight: 3,150 pounds
Payload (with full fuel): 285 pounds
Seats: 4
Cruise speed: 10 miles per hour
Highlights: It was popular in the 1950s and has a roomy cabin, mostly suited for summer seasonal work on lakes with plenty of space for takeoff.

A family enjoys some time off in a Gullwing Stinson somewhere in Alaska during the 1940s. After World War II, private recreational use of aircraft became more commonplace. New opportunities opened up for bush services that catered to an increasing number of recreational wilderness tourists.

Braun went back to reclaim his snubbed fish, and the bear came. It could move at very high speed when it so desired. Braun made another sprint for the SeaBee with the trout, lunch box, and coffee pot in hand, and he made a mad scramble aboard to safety at last. By this time, the bear was lounging on the beach as if it were watching the Sunday matinee, agape at the human hijinks around it, and too bemused to wave as the SeaBee and the lunch box rattled off into the blue.

Braun's job as chief pilot for Wardair, founded by Max Ward, one of Canada's most colorful aviation entrepreneurs, kept him servicing the northern mines and settlements around the clock, six days a week. His weekend family sojourns in his own airplane were equally representative of how economic change and advances in aviation changed wilderness flying.

During the postwar years, aviation became ingrained in the bush as a way of life. The war had brought a comprehensive aviation infrastructure where there was practically none before. The long economic boom of the 1950s generated a seemingly insatiable demand for natural resources and the services of bushplanes to help extract them. The availability of thousands of war surplus airplanes suitable for service in the bush and the commitment of governments to improve access to isolated bush settlements also brought regular, reliable air service to local communities on an unprecedented scale.

de Havilland DHC-3 Otter

Year introduced: 1951

Engine: 600-horsepower Pratt and Whitney R-1340

Fuel: 215 gallons

Gross weight: 8,000 pounds

Payload (with full fuel): 2,000 pounds

Seats: 16

Cruise speed: 140 miles per hour

Highlights: The Beaver's big brother, the Otter, had excellent STOL performance to overcome the drawbacks of less-than-ideal engine power.

The media actively encouraged the recreational use of airplanes in the 1940s, including adventure travel. A 1947 edition of *Canadian Aviation* shows the versatility of amphibians, such as this Grumman Mallard, for personal bush use.

One Canadian company, de Havilland Canada (DHC), introduced two aircraft designed specifically for wilderness flying in the 1950s. The Beaver and the Otter became synonymous with the term *bushplane*. The effort of other aircraft makers to find postwar civilian markets to offset the precipitous loss of wartime business brought other benefits to the wilderness. They relied on the emergence of a new family of dependable small aircraft engines and developed a whole new class of small, capable, and relatively inexpensive airplanes, many of them ideal for the bush.

Individuals who were not primarily pilots, but had pilot's licenses, bought these aircraft in large numbers and used them in the bush as their contemporaries used automobiles in more refined surroundings. Doctors, accountants, salesmen, lawyers, professional guides, priests, and others flew themselves in increasing numbers on their business rounds during the week and headed for their favorite hunting, fishing, or scenic canoeing or hiking spots for the weekend. By the 1950s, 1 in 50 Alaskans was a pilot, more than 10 times the rate for the whole United States.

A strange new kind of aircraft made its debut in the wilderness, the helicopter. It was viewed with suspicion by most bush pilots, but enthusiastically embraced by a select few. Helicopters are much more expensive to operate than comparable fixed-wing bushplanes and initially unable to carry much of a load, but they carved out an important niche for themselves and left ample scope for the longevity of the traditional bushplane.

The economic boom also created, for the first time, a large middle class with money to spend on more than just the bare necessities. Recreational travel, once the preserve of the rich, was poised to become a middle-class passion, and as economies of scale kicked in, a big business. A trickle of tourists and adventure travelers to the northern wilderness turned into a flood and provided a major new market for bush-flying services. Flying in and supporting fishing and hunting parties and hauling tourists to wilderness lodges above the spectacular scenery became primary sources of employment for many bush pilots.

As the cold war accelerated into high gear, bush pilots found ample opportunity to play their part as they had in World War II and provided support for the DEW line (the Distant Early Warning

The Republic SeaBee was a postwar personal amphibian that many bush operators used for light duties. The verdict was mixed. Everyone agreed it was underpowered with its 215-horsepower Franklin engine, but some found its large cabin appealing and it was widely used in summer operations.

radar chain to alert the United States and Canada to approaching hostile aircraft across the Arctic) and other military installations and activities.

The founders of several of Alaska's larger bush-flying services were driven by ambitions to build scheduled airlines operating large, modern airliners. With the infrastructure in place and surplus transport aircraft available at bargain prices after World War II, they were able to achieve their aspirations. As surplus DC-3s and other larger aircraft joined their lines, their operations acquired an airline division and a bush division. The airline division had regular schedules on the trunk lines between a set of hubs, and the bush division offered scheduled services the old-fashioned way in bushplanes to the dozens of outlying settlements scattered around the hubs. This was the structure of Wien Alaska Airlines, Northern Consolidated Airlines, Pacific Northern Airlines, Reeve Aleutian Airways, and Cordova Airlines.

Room for Entrepreneurs

There continued to be opportunities for entrepreneurial self-starters to get into the business. Any motivated commercial pilot with a plane could start a charter or air taxi business and see what he could make of it.

Alaska Airlines was taken over by New York City-based investors during World War II and went on after the war to operate mostly large equipment. It started with DC-3s, DC-4s, and C-46s and dived headlong into the global nonscheduled business under several adventurous and financially none-too-astute managers. Its escapades around the world during the late 1940s and 1950s makes Archie Satterfield's history of the airline, *The Alaska Airlines Story*, read like a thriller, but the company largely got out of the small airplane bush-flying business, except for occasional ad hoc opportunities and during transition periods when it took over a smaller operator to acquire its routes. Its chief Alaskan interest was securing a coveted route to the lower 48 states, which it finally achieved in 1951 with a temporary certificate to fly the Portland-Seattle-Fairbanks-Anchorage route, which was made permanent in 1957.

Wien Alaska Airlines was a different story. Its bush division remained a pillar of its operations to the end. Its airline division's first large aircraft were DC-3s that were flown between its Fairbanks, Nome, and Barrow hubs with interim stops, from where a bush air force scattered passengers to points farther afield. The operation run by James "Andy" Anderson from Bettles, a stop on the three-times-a-week DC-3 run between Fairbanks and Barrow, was typical of the bush-flying arm.

Anderson, a World War II Navy carrier pilot, signed on with Wien in 1950 and was initially given a two-seat Cessna 140 to service the Koyukuk Valley. For years he was a one-pilot show, lived in a pair of tents at Bettles Field, and paid out of his own pocket for the materials to construct a permanent building as the Alaskan winter approached. As respected as Wien's operation was, the company terminally sailed close to financial disaster and often passed the pressure on to its employees. Anderson finally was repaid for the building in company stock.

Anderson's flights were typical bush pilot missions: mail and grocery flights to the local communities and mines, medical emergency flights, charters with miners, prospectors, government officials, and fly fishermen, hunters, and their guides. He also flew wildlife film makers who frequently showed up in Alaska to feed television's voraciously growing appetite for nature documentaries.

Anderson's Cessna 140 was one of Cessna's first light aircraft with a horizontally opposed four-cylinder air-cooled engine that created a lighter category of aircraft than those powered by the heavy radial engines of the 1930s and 1940s. Although the 140 was small and limited to light loads, Cessna's bigger, more powerful high-wing tail-draggers that soon followed—the Cessna 170, 180, and 185—were good, light bush aircraft suited for carrying small parties on wheels, skis, and floats and making supply runs when demand was insufficient to justify a larger aircraft. The Cessna 185 still soldiers on, along with several later types of these capable high-wing utility aircraft.

Over 17 years of flying for Wien, Anderson flew his share of bush aircraft, including the Cessna 180, Noorduyn Norseman, Beaver, Otter, and Beech 18. He was instrumental in convincing the airline to buy the Swiss Pilatus Porter for its bush division in the 1960s. Of all the airplanes he flew, there was only one that Anderson really disliked, the Republic SeaBee, and he wasn't alone in his opinion.

Pilatus PC-6 Turbo Porter

Year introduced: 1965
Engine: 680-horsepower Pratt and Whitney Canada PT6
Fuel: 170 gallons
Gross weight: 6,100 pounds
Payload (with full fuel): 2,000 pounds
Seats: 10
Cruise speed: 140 miles per hour
Highlights: It is a perfect example of expensive, helicopter-like, precision Swiss engineering. It is popular with Wien Air and Air America.

Rugged Individualists

Several of Alaska's bush operators built their own business from modest beginnings into a major operation without merging with other companies. Few did it as well as Jim and Dottie Magoffin, founders of Interior Airways. They launched their business in Fairbanks with a single Taylorcraft as a hunting and fishing guide service in 1946. Within a few years they had a small bush fleet, including a Howard DGA, a Cessna 170, and an Aeronca Air Sedan. Their big break came when they were awarded a contract to support the construction of the DEW line throughout the Arctic. The Magoffins snapped up any suitable aircraft they could get to fulfill the ambitious contract, and Interior Airways soon resembled a flying bushplane museum with its 1929 Travelair 6000, 1933 Stinson SR, 1943 Grumman Widgeon, Beech C-45s, and Noorduyn Norseman. Bigger aircraft also joined the fleet, including four C-46 Curtiss Commandos.

Building on its Arctic experience, Interior Airways expanded into passenger services with Lockheed Constellations and F-27 turboprops. The major oil discovery on the North Slope and its development on a massive scale needed massive air support, and Interior Airways was there to help. By the late 1960s, Interior Airways flew heavy-lift C-82 Flying Boxcars and a fleet of Lockheed C-130 cargo aircraft.

Interior Airways' C-130s supported the construction of the 600-mile-long Alaska oil pipeline from Prudhoe Bay to Valdez.

The company is also remembered for SAG WON, the airport it built in a strategically located spot in the middle of nowhere in the Brooks Range. The airport became a hub for the aerial support of the Alaskan oil rush. The name is derived from two rivers near the 6,500-foot strip.

As the Trans-Alaska pipeline experienced years of delays, the Magoffins renamed their airline Alaska International Air and hauled cargo worldwide in their C-130s until the pipeline project got back on track. The Magoffins retired in 1982 and the airline became Markair and flew jets as far as New York. It is gone now, consumed by the turbulence in the airline industry in the 1990s, but an Interior Airlines Noorduyn Norseman can still be seen at the Alaska Aviation Heritage Museum in Anchorage.

The SeaBee's streamlined, art deco curves and egg-shaped, spacious cabin looked elegant enough and it perfectly fit the "airplane in every garage" image heavily promoted by the aircraft manufacturers after the war. But it also had a cranky 215-horsepower Franklin engine in pusher configuration aft of the cabin that was too feeble to effectively haul the airplane's legal gross weight, let alone the overloads that bush pilots routinely stuffed into their mounts. On water it had a comparatively long

takeoff run, and it was difficult to preheat its rear-mounted engine. Wardair's chief pilot, Don Braun, thought it was a satisfactory private airplane, suitable for family trips, and he was careful to pamper the engine to avoid trouble. The SeaBee also was fine for some seasonal summer niches, and quite a few were used in commercial operations but didn't stand up well to heavy-duty bush wear. Anderson was ready to trade in his SeaBee after one particularly disconcerting experience with its doggy performance.

The incident happened on a trip to an Inuit summer camp on a small lake in the Anaktuvuk Pass in the Brooks Range. On departure, the lackadaisical airplane didn't make it without any headwind on a length of water Anderson thought was marginally adequate for takeoff. Its hull was gouged on a hidden rock at the end of the lake, and a wingtip float was broken on the trees bordering it.

Determined to fly the plane home, Anderson borrowed a dogsled runner and used it as a splint to reattach the float. He asked the Inuits how they'd fix a hole in one of their boats. They melted 5 pounds of Caribou fat, soaked rags in it, and stuffed them into the hole. After the patch hardened, Anderson was able to coax the thankless amphibian back to Bettles.

The Grumman Goose

Another amphibian of the 1940s fared much better than the SeaBee in Alaska and it achieved a cult following among its most dedicated fans. It was the squat, twin-engine, eight-passenger Grumman Goose, and it thrived in the southeast. The first Goose showed up in the Gastineau Channel and sidled up to the Juneau seaplane dock on Valentine's Day 1945. It was fresh out of the Royal Canadian

Many bush services expanded into more elaborate airline operations following World War II and were helped by the ready, inexpensive availability of surplus transport aircraft, such as the Douglas DC-3. These aircraft transformed Mudhole Smith's Cordova Airlines from a bush operation into a substantial airline. In spite of all the airports built in the bush during the war, not all landing fields changed with the times.

Wien Alaska Airlines became a major airline after World War II and heavily promoted Arctic tourism. Wien was among the operators to own and run its own lodges at its more attractive tourist destinations.

Canadian Pacific President Grant McConachie didn't wait for long after the war to realize his lifelong ambition of running a major airline. In spite of the monopoly on the choice routes, the government formed a national carrier, Trans Canada Air Lines, which was later renamed Air Canada. By 1950, Canadian Pacific flew to the Far East and Australia, in addition to its extensive domestic bush network.

Air Force, from whom Shell Simmons had bought it in Vancouver, British Columbia, for Alaska Coastal Airlines. By the late 1950s Alaska Coastal Airlines flew eight of the powerful amphibians.

Alaska Coastal's chief competitor, Bob Ellis' Ellis Air Transport, wasn't far behind and bought its first Goose later in 1945. By 1947 Ellis operated three of them, and within a decade the Goose fleet rose to nine.

Ellis Air Transport had a novel use for its Gooses at Ketchikan. The town was served by an airport on dry land capable of accommodating large airliners, but the field was on Annette Island, 21 miles away by water. Every incoming airliner was met by Ellis' amphibians, which landed on wheels at Annette Island and whisked arriving passengers to the downtown Ketchikan waterfront in a 12-minute flight. "What...no landing field?" was Ellis Air Transport's advertising slogan for the service. The pilots took great care to explain to incoming passengers that the splash at Ketchikan was not a crash, but a normal landing on water.

Ellis also ran the shuttle with a PBY Catalina from 1959 and carried as many as 24 passengers. Ellis' amphibians also took passengers to other regional destinations from Annette Island. The service went on until 1973 when Ketchikan's own current jet port was completed. By then Ellis had merged with Alaska Coastal Airlines, and the merged company had been part of Alaska Airlines for five years.

The Goose was perfectly suited for the needs of the southeast, where water-based bush flying remained the norm because the few strategic airfields of World War II, with the exception of Juneau, had to be built far from major settlements for the lack of easily accessible flat land anywhere else. Even Juneau's airport experienced a temporary setback when Pan American introduced the Lockheed Constellation and announced it was moving its Juneau stop to the ex-military field of not-so-nearby Gustavus until the Juneau airport was brought up to standards to accommodate the new propliner.

Pilots, like Bill Stedman of Petersburg, Alaska, who flew the Goose for more than two decades for Alaska Coastal Airways and Petersburg-based Alaska Island Airlines, loved the airplane. The combined 900 horsepower of its Pratt & Whitney engines provided plenty of power. It practically couldn't be overloaded, it was as stable as a rock in flight, and it performed well in rough water. The airplane would fly with whatever fit inside it. It could also cruise at speeds up to 160 knots, fast even today for an amphibian or a floatplane.

While free of major vices, the Goose had a few quirks. It could be tricky on wheeled landings because of its narrow wheelbase and tail-dragger layout. The two engines provided plenty of power, but not the comfortable twin-engine redundancy as might be expected. Because of the aircraft's stocky, drag-inducing airframe, if a Goose suffered an engine failure and was carrying anything but the lightest load, it was unlikely to be able to maintain level flight and most likely faced a crash landing if no waterway or airport was nearby. The high reliability of the 450-horsepower Pratt & Whitneys offset the risk.

Stedman never experienced a serious incident with the Goose, but he did have his share of adventures in it. The strangest among them was a landing at Big Port Water near a fish-processing plant on a turbulent day. He was wary of the landing on the relatively unsheltered stretch of water, but examined the water surface carefully and decided it was marginally calm enough to land. He made a long, straight-in approach, but on touchdown, the Goose was banged around so hard that he feared he would lose it. It took a while for the startled pilot to realize that a heavy layer of herring oil from the fish processing plant coated the water surface and suppressed the whitecaps on top of the waves that would indicate the water was too rough to land. Stedman was grateful to have been in the sturdy Goose on the flight.

Alaska Island Airlines of Petersburg, with whom Stedman flew for 16 years, was one of dozens of small Alaskan air services that offered charters and air taxis after World War II. They filled a niche alongside the bigger airlines. With three Cessna 180s, a Beaver, and the Goose, Alaska Island Airlines resembled the traditional small bush services of the 1930s. It flourished with the old-fashioned on-demand flights that were always the essence of bush flying.

Don Bedford also remembers the Grumman Goose with affection. They were excellent performers, easy to work on, and rarely required more than routine care. The PBY Catalina was another matter. Bedford and his colleagues had to look after a fleet of as many as five PBYs, and the big amphibian took up a disproportionate amount of their time. Difficult access to the PBY's engines was the least of their problems, as treacherous as it was to climb up to access them on icy days. Designed to drone along at a steady pace for as much as 22 hours on long-range naval patrols, the average bush hop for a PBY in the southeast was 25 minutes and this gave an unsustainable beating to its original Wright 1820 engines. The civilian operators couldn't afford to throw away the engines after 300 hours like the Navy. Most PBYs had their engines upgraded to the more powerful Wright 2600s, which was a big improvement.

This Wien map and Reeve Aleutian passenger ID tag show some of the scope of scheduled airline services throughout Alaska by the 1950s. Airliners may have been flying them, but bush pilots pioneered them. The smaller destinations were served by bush divisions of the airlines and independent operators.

In its own class, the Cessna 185 is as enduring as the de Havilland Beaver. It has plenty of power and load-bearing ability for its size.

107

Ellis Air Transport of Ketchikan was quick to step up to the Grumman Goose. The company bought its first war surplus Goose at the end of 1945, and it operated nine of them within a decade.

The Ellis Air Transport logo captures the atmosphere of its operating environment.

Introducing the Helicopter

A good bushplane's greatest strength is its ability to squeeze in and out of the tightest fields or smallest lakes with a useful load to easily and rapidly access the most remote locations. Ever since the earliest sorties of the Canadian flying boats over the wilderness, a bushplane's competition was another bushplane. By the late 1940s as the helicopter was coming of age, that was about to change.

The first hint of these toy-like rotorcrafts' potential came in 1944 when a primitive Sikorsky helicopter, reminiscent of a pesky mosquito, rescued critically injured soldiers deep in the Burmese jungle from a clearing barely wider than the diameter of its rotor blades. No bushplane would have been able to perform the rescue for the lack of a landing area within practical reach large enough for a fixed-wing aircraft. Without the helicopter, the men would have died.

The helicopter had a slow start in wilderness flying because of a fundamental weakness and several other shortcomings. The early piston engine–powered helicopters were woefully underpowered, so they were of little use when the name of the game was to lift the heftiest load possible. Helicopters were also very expensive. Operating costs were high and the helicopter's range was limited. It was uncompetitive with fixed-wing bushplanes, but all it takes is a foothold to give a promising emerging technology a chance to realize its potential. That is what Carl Agar did in 1949 in British Columbia's Okanogan region, although he didn't see it that way at the time because he was preoccupied with trying to make a living.

Agar and some partners managed a meager existence with a small flying school when crop-dusting experiments with Bell 47 helicopters in nearby Washington state gave him the idea to spray the Okanogan's fruit orchards. They acquired a Bell 47 with the assistance of the orchard growers, formed Okanogan Helicopters, and found out that orchard dusting in the Okanogan was a bust because the orchards were too small and mixed for aerial spraying to be effective.

Okanogan Helicopters needed new opportunities and found one hauling surveyors around the nearby mountains. The helicopters could drop off and pick up their passengers right where the surveyors wanted to go instead of having to hike from the nearest landing area for fixed-wing aircraft, and their deep-pocketed employers were happy to pay the bills. Agar became quite a rotary-wing mountain pilot. He quickly discovered that at higher altitudes, the best place to land was a precarious ledge with a steep drop because on take-off he had to roll the anemic Bell off the ledge down into the void to pick up a safe flying speed.

Rather than supplanting bushplanes, the early helicopters complemented them quite well under the right circumstances. The less expensive, more capable bushplanes would provide service as close to a wilderness site as possible, then helicopters could shuttle personnel and supplies to their final destination.

The Grumman Goose survives mainly in the hands of private owners as a lavishly restored antique, such as this example seen over the Atlantic Ocean. They can also still be found sporadically in commercial service along the coast of British Columbia. The Goose uses basically the same engine as the Beaver, but less than 350 aircraft were built and spare parts can be a problem. Serious antique restorers spare no expense making what parts they can't find, but that doesn't make economic sense for commercial operators.

Okanogan's clients were enthusiastic helicopter converts. In 1951 the Aluminum Company of Canada (Alcan) built the biggest privately funded hydroelectric dam in the world, and the young helicopter company ensured its future when it received a major contract to provide support services. In addition to the Bell 47s, the deep-pocketed Alcan also bought larger, more capable Sikorsky S-55 helicopters.

The helicopters were also gradually and selectively used for some tasks in the logging and forestry industry, and following the Alcan project, Okanogan thrived for years by supporting the construction of the Mid-Canada chain of the DEW Line and added Sikorsky S-58s to its fleet. Except for occasional use by well-financed companies, the expensive helicopter remained largely absent from wilderness flying until the introduction of the turbine helicopter in the 1960s, which laid to rest any payload questions by being able to lift its own weight.

Carl Agar founded Okanogan Helicopters in part because of the intense competition in the traditional fixed-wing general aviation field in postwar Canada. Pilots were a dime a dozen and anyone could scrape together the few dollars or the credit required to buy a surplus Tiger Moth or Avro Anson and start a flying school or charter business. Shoestring operators sprouted up everywhere, including the bush country, and were determined to make it alongside the big players. They faced quite a challenge for growing beyond their small operations in Canada's highly restrictive air transport environment. The government continued to hold its monopoly on all the mainline routes through its ownership and subsidy of Trans Canada Air Lines. The bigger national and regional private operators, such as Canadian Airways and Vancouver-based Queen Charlotte Airlines, dominated the rest of the industry.

The first few postwar years were tough economically, in spite of a great deal of hope for better times. As the economy began to pick up by the beginning of the 1950s, the extractive industries swung into high gear and the prospects of bush operators, large and small, improved. Their chances received a boost when the Canadian government, buoyed by a profound sense of postwar optimism,

A Grumman Mallard is shown in a picture postcard setting that is the norm in Alaska. Equipped with two inline Ranger piston engines, it was underpowered and operators invariably preferred the larger, more powerful Goose if they could afford it. This Mallard's pilot improvised a novel sea anchor by extending the wheels.

poured money into developing the country's remotest regions and the civilian aviation infrastructure to support it.

Many of the weaker air service operators that formed after the war were soon gone, but others who had the business acumen to match their commitment to flying made the most of their opportunities. Among them was Russ Baker, who founded Central BC Airways in Fort Saint James and expanded it to Kamloops, where he faced competition from a handful of other small operators. Baker's key to survival was his ability to secure the regional flying contract from the BC Forestry Service. He then cheerfully drove his competitors out of business in a rather ruthless manner at times.

One competitor who operated with a single SeaBee recalled one of the ambitious entrepreneur's favorite tactics. Baker would wait until the competitor's airplane was out on a charter and would have an accomplice call the operator to demand to be taken somewhere immediately. The request, of course, had to be refused and Baker instantly fired off an indignant letter to the authorities complaining that the competitor wasn't able to meet demand for charter services and Baker's Central BC Airways should immediately receive additional charter permits. Eventually the competitor sold out to Baker.

Baker was most interested in acquiring weaker operators to get their route authorizations. He took over Associated Air Taxi's business to get a foothold in the key market of Vancouver. Central BC Airways was renamed Pacific Western Airlines in 1953 to better reflect its ambitions. It then acquired Queen Charlotte Airlines, which brought coveted scheduled services and Associated

Airways, which led to a lucrative DEW Line support contract. Baker died in 1958, but by then the airline he built was well on its way to becoming Canada's third largest air carrier. By the 1980s, it was able to acquire Canadian Pacific Airlines and Wardair, both major airlines by then, which had their roots in bush flying.

There was a silver lining for entry-level bush operators struggling to compete against established firms. As the bigger outfits pushed themselves to grow into mainstream airlines, they eventually shed their bush operations and created new opportunities for the smaller players. But small fry or large, Canadian or American, when air service operators wanted to add a new bushplane to their fleet in the late 1940s, they most hankered for the de Havilland Beaver, one of Canada's most lasting contributions to bush flying.

The Beaver

The Beaver began as one of several pending projects de Havilland Canada considered in the waning months of World War II to replace the firm's wartime military contracts. De Havilland built more than 1,100 twin-engine Mosquito bombers during the war. Its story is brilliantly told by Sean Rossiter in the Beaver's definitive history, *The Immortal Beaver: The World's Best Bush Plane*.

The DHC-2 Beaver was inspired by de Havilland's managing director, Phil Garratt, who had been moved upstairs into Toronto's tallest skyscraper during the middle of the war to

de Havilland DHC-2 Beaver

Year introduced: 1947
Engine: 450-horsepower Pratt and Whitney R-985
Fuel: 95 gallons
Gross weight: 5,090 pounds
Payload (with full fuel): 1,000 pounds
Seats: 7
Cruise speed: 100 miles per hour
Highlights: Many consider it to be the best bushplane made. Production ended in 1967 and 1,631 total were built. More than 1,000 are still in service today.

free the vastly growing company from his antiquated prewar day-to-day management style. He was let out of the skyscraper to run the company again after the war, but during the war he was charged with doing the strategic planning for DHC's postwar future. One of the projects he envisioned was an all-metal bushplane with a 4,000-pound gross weight and the ability to carry a 1,000-pound load. Its most important attribute would be one most desired by bush operators, the ability to take off and land in much shorter distances than any competing aircraft. It was a Short Takeoff and Landing airplane long before the acronym STOL came into use.

The Piper Cubs immediately found acceptance in the bush with their light airframes and, in the case of the Super Cub, a powerful 150- to 180-horsepower Lycoming engine that enabled it to go, land, and get out of anywhere. Many Super Cubs are still flown by hunting and fishing guide services, wildlife management agencies, and private owners.

This trapper and his family are photographed with the Stinson that made their livelihood possible. The ability to have a wider range and regularly retrieve valuable furs from the bush in high volume allowed airplanes to significantly increase the level of business fur trappers could conduct.

An all-metal STOL airplane designed specifically for the bush was long overdue, given the punishment wooden components can suffer in the harsh, extreme wilderness. Airframe deterioration from the constant humidity, moisture, and temperature changes was not unusual, especially in the wooden wings still prevalent in many light aircraft at the time. While metal is subject to corrosion, the risk is much less and easily managed. Based on experience, Jack Jefford of the Alaska Region CAA would have given his strongest endorsement to Phil Garratt's all-metal idea had he been aware of it.

Jefford was at a party when one of his mechanics burst in and told him that he had just crashed a truck into the wing of one of the agency's twin Cessnas and severely damaged the plane. The easygoing Jefford soothed the mechanic's ruffled nerves and drove to the airport with him to take a look. When he peered into the opened-up wing, he discovered that the inside structure was disastrously infested with wood rot. He cracked open the other wing and it was just as bad. Somehow water had seeped into the wings for a long time and didn't drain or dry out. Jefford doubted that the spars would have lasted the coming week, during which he was scheduled to fly the airplane.

Don Bedford of Alaska Coastal Airlines saw firsthand a less threatening, routine drawback to wooden airframes. By late fall every year, the wooden wings of the company's Lockheed Vegas weighed a third more than in the spring from all the moisture they had absorbed during the summer season. Bedford had to haul the wings up into the heated hangar's rafters to dry them out over the winter.

Ellis Air Transport's chief rival, Alaska Coastal Airlines of Juneau, also operated the Grumman Goose as the main type in its fleet, and when the two companies merged in 1962, the combined airline had the biggest Goose fleet in the world. Boarding a Goose was not always easy, depending on docking conditions.

How They Compare

When clients hire a bushplane, two of the most common questions asked are how much load can it carry and how fast can it get it there. Payload is the weight the airplane can carry beyond the weight of the crew and fuel. In the figures below, a full fuel load is assumed. Another useful indicator of bush performance is power loading, which is gross weight divided by horsepower. It tells us how many pounds each horsepower has to lift when the airplane is fully loaded. The less weight per horsepower, the higher the performance.

While power loading is a good initial guide to how well an airplane will perform, the lift characteristics of the wing and other factors also have a lot to do with how well an airplane will climb and how long its takeoff and landing distances will be. The STOL winged Beaver has one of the lowest power loadings and gains additional advantage from its STOL wing. Compare its wing loading to the Fairchild Husky, which lost out to the Beaver on performance, even though it could lift a greater load and cruised faster.

Note the difference in power loading between the Noorduyn Norseman Mark I with the 420-horsepower engine, and the Mark IV, the same airplane re-engined with the 600-horsepower engine. While the Mark IV's power loading equals the Beaver's and exceeds the Otter's, its airfoil and flap system is not as advanced and makes it less of a STOL performer.

Interior Airways' C-130s supported the construction of the 600-mile-long Alaska oil pipeline from Prudhoe Bay to Valdez.

	Payload (lb)	Power Loading (gross weight/hp)	Cruise Speed (mph)
HS-2L Curtiss Flying Boat	800	16.0	65
Fokker Super Universal	600	8.7	98
Noorduyn Norseman MK I	1,600	14.2	120
Noorduyn Norseman MK IV	1,500	11.0	140
DHC-2 Beaver	1,000	11.1	100
Fairchild Husky	1,400	14.0	123
DHC-3 Otter	2,000	13.3	140
Piper Super Cub	429	11.7	115
Fairchild 71	1,000	14.2	95
Cessna 206	975	11.6	166

A main use for Ellis' aircraft was to ferry passengers that arrived by air at Ketchikan from the airport on Annette Island, 21 miles away by air, to the Ketchikan waterfront.

Big users of aircraft in the wilderness are the various wildlife management agencies, such as the Department of Interior's Fish and Wildlife Service. Their aerial activities include wildlife surveys, migration tracking, fish stocking, moving wildlife that has become a danger to the local community, and other tasks.

The Beaver's concept design was created by Wsiewolod Jakimiuk, de Havilland Canada's chief design engineer. When he escaped to Canada from his native Poland before the German invasion in World War II, Jakimiuk was already a world-class aeronautical engineer. He was a founder of the PZL aircraft factory and a pioneering designer of all-metal aircraft. Concurrent with developing the Beaver concept, he designed DHC's first postwar aircraft, the graceful and wildly successful DHC-1 Chipmunk military trainer that replaced the Tiger Moth.

Jakimiuk was an interesting choice to do the concept design of a muscle plane like the Beaver. Like most European aeronautical engineers, he believed in doing more with elegant aerodynamics than brute engine power. In fact, his concept drawings show a sleek, all-metal aircraft with a cantilever wing (no struts) and a gracefully pointy nose concealing an inline 300-horsepower de Havilland engine that was being developed by de Havilland, DHC's parent company, in the United Kingdom.

As Rossiter's extensive research reveals, Jakimiuk's aerodynamics-over-power approach to the Beaver's design may have inadvertently led to its perfection in an indirect fashion. The detail design was handed off to two up-and-coming aeronautical engineers, Fred Buller, who became the Beaver project's chief engineer, and Dick Hiscocks, its aerodynamicist.

Upon a review of the work completed, Hiscocks realized that the Beaver, which at that time was provisionally called the DHC-X, would be quite underpowered. He was particularly concerned about takeoff performance, especially on floats. DHC's British parent company was imperially insisting on the 330-horsepower engine it was developing in spite of the thousands of surplus 450-horsepower U.S. Pratt & Whitney radials available for a pittance. Hiscocks did the best thing he could as an aerodynamicist. He improved the wing's aerodynamics for short field performance to the best of his abilities, which turned out to be rather a lot.

He changed the airfoil to one that generated higher lift and designed the ailerons to droop down with the slotted flaps for additional lift. He also reduced weight in the wing by going to a strut-supported design, although the main motivation for the struts was to allow for a thinner spar that allowed more headroom in the cabin. Buller worked closely with Hiscocks and detail designed the structures that would efficiently accomplish the aerodynamicist's specifications.

The pair doubted they could obtain decent performance out of the airplane, even with all the design improvements, until they received the break that was the making of the Beaver. The parent company's engine blew up on the test bench and DHC decided to make a stand. The Beaver received the 450-horsepower Pratt & Whitney it deserved. The design team widened the fuselage to accommodate the heavier, but proportionally more powerful, engine (and gain extra cargo space), upped the gross weight to 5,000 pounds, strengthened the wing to support the engine, extended the landing gear to accommodate the bigger prop, and the rest is history.

The Beaver had its first flight on August 16, 1947. Well before its first flight, Punch Dickins joined DHC as the Beaver's principal salesman. By the time it went out of production, 1,631 were built. All production piston Beavers were Mark Is and there was never a need for a new, improved model. A single Beaver was re-engined with a 550-horsepower British Alves Leonides engine for evaluation by the RAF and was called Mark II for the trials, but the service decided to stick to the Pratt & Whitney–powered Mark I model. The only other Beaver was the Turbo Beaver, referred to as the Mark III, and 60 were built in the 1960s before all Beaver production ceased in 1968.

The Ontario Provincial Air Service was the Beaver's launch customer and needed 25 aircraft. OPAS ordered 12 Beavers to begin with and selected it over the Fairchild Husky, which had been completed a year earlier. The Husky was a considerably bigger, heavier airplane powered by the same 450-horsepower Pratt & Whitney used on the Beaver. If the Husky had benefited from Hiscocks' and Buller's talent, it would have undoubtedly received a higher performance wing and the 600-horsepower engine it deserved, with interesting implications for the Otter. Following the loss of OPAS' order, only 11 Huskies were built. Some were re-engined and several of them flew for decades.

An initially unanticipated customer for the Beaver purchased the largest number of them. A total of 976 Beavers served in the U.S. armed forces, and most were assigned to the Army. Such a large figure may seem surprising today, but the helicopter hadn't come into its own and the Beaver proved to be the ultimate fixed-wing frontline utility and liaison aircraft. Scores of Beavers served in the Korean War by the second half of 1951.

The Beaver was such a hit with bush operators that the company sold the prototype. It was an uncharacteristic step for an aircraft manufacturer, but the persuasive buyer, Russ Baker of Central BC Airways, was in a bind. Three of his aircraft had crashed in quick succession just as he secured the Forestry Service contract that kept his company alive. Reneging on the contract would be the end of his dreams of a bush-flying empire even before he began to build one.

Baker didn't know the meaning of the word *renege*, but he was having trouble thinking his way out of his predicament when Punch Dickins appeared in the Beaver prototype he was using as a demonstrator. A check on the spot from Baker's skeptical financial backer convinced a reluctant Dickins to part with the aircraft, the sixth Beaver to be delivered. Baker had a narrow escape. Better still, the Beaver's amazing productivity put the budding bush-flying empire right back on track, and more. After 32 years of commercial service, the prototype Beaver finally took its well-earned place in the Canada Aviation Museum in Ottawa.

The DHC-3 Otter

The Beaver was a tough act to follow, but that is exactly what DHC intended to do. Almost immediately after the Beaver's introduction, bush customers expressed a strong interest in an airplane that could haul twice the payload with similar short takeoff and landing performance. The Ontario Provincial Air Service was particularly interested because it was making good progress in developing the technical capability of using aircraft floats as a fire bombing platform

Today helicopters perform a variety of bush missions for which they are better suited than fixed-wing aircraft. A helicopter (the tiny dot next to the yellow tent) has landed and supports a scientific team on this glacier on a spot off-limits for fixed-wing aircraft. Helicopters and airplanes cooperate on search missions, but the actual rescue is normally done by the helicopter.

The helicopter had a modest beginning in bush flying, but even the earliest, most underpowered models could go places and complete tasks no fixed-wing aircraft was capable of performing. Okanogan Helicopters of Vancouver, British Columbia, introduced rotary-wing flying to the bush in the late 1940s with a tiny Bell 47 that picked up surveyors where the bushplanes had to drop them and took them directly to their job sites.

Many consider the de Havilland DHC-2 Beaver the greatest bushplane of all time. Its STOL capability in conjunction with its 1,000-pound payload is unmatched. Even though these planes were introduced in 1947, more than a thousand still are flying today.

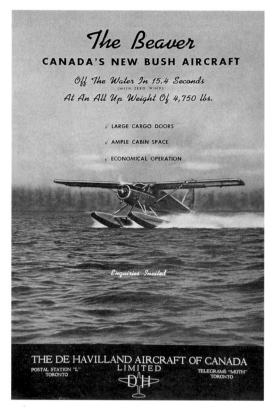

The Beaver
CANADA'S NEW BUSH AIRCRAFT

Off The Water In 15.4 Seconds
(WITH ZERO WIND)
At An All Up Weight Of 4,750 lbs.

√ LARGE CARGO DOORS
√ AMPLE CABIN SPACE
√ ECONOMICAL OPERATION

Enquiries Invited

THE DE HAVILLAND AIRCRAFT OF CANADA
LIMITED
POSTAL STATION "L"   TELEGRAMS "MOTH"
TORONTO   TORONTO

The Beaver didn't need a slick advertising campaign. A persuasive operator in British Columbia who had suffered three aircraft crashes in quick succession managed to persuade de Havilland to sell him the prototype Beaver.

and was willing to commit to an order of 20 aircraft that could carry the required payload. The Royal Canadian Air Force was also interested in replacing its Norseman fleet with a more capable aircraft. There was also the U.S. Army, although its Beaver orders were still relatively modest at this time. A DHC design team, led by the Beaver's principal designers, began detailed work on the new project in 1950. The aircraft was tentatively called the King Beaver and became the DHC-3 Otter.

The Otter was often referred to as an upscale Beaver and implied a commonality of elements, but it was designed from scratch based on the same principles. Dick Hiscocks was responsible for the aerodynamics of the project and tackled the wing with the same zeal to maximize its STOL performance that he applied to the Beaver's design. He also faced the same challenge he had encountered in the Beaver's initial design phase, an engine that was less powerful than ideal for what it was being asked to do. This time there was no last-minute upgrade to a more powerful engine because none were available. Delivering the performance margin that would mean the difference between success and mediocrity would be up to the wing.

The engine selected was the 600-horsepower Pratt & Whitney R-1340 because there was no other option between the smaller 450-horsepower radial and the 1,000-plus-horsepower engines that powered the large multi-engined aircraft of the day. These engines weren't widely available at the time, and most of them still served the airplanes they were built for, which were yet to be surplussed. DHC scoured the world for a suitable version of the engine and came up with a batch of 50 to start production. Availability later eased as more engines were surplussed and DHC contracted Pratt & Whitney to rebuild them to factory-new standards for the Otters.

The Otter's wing design surpassed the Beaver's to deliver stellar STOL performance. The high-lift airfoil's performance is maximized by flaps that run the entire length of the wing's trailing edge. Inboard double-slotted flaps come down 60 degrees, and the double-slotted arrangement allows air to flow between the two flap sections to generate additional lift. The outboard sections of the flaps double as ailerons and droop 26 degrees when full flaps are selected.

Flown conservatively on its first flight on December 12, 1951, the Otter leapt into the air in less than 600 feet and ascended in a climb that was compared to an elevator ride. Within weeks it impressed VIPs by taking off and landing in under 100 feet in a good headwind with a light load, and climbed in excess of 1,000 feet per minute.

In the field, the Otter quickly proved its mettle. The wheeled version at gross weight was routinely off in calm conditions at sea level in 600 feet, less with any headwind, and achieved a 1,000–feet-per-minute initial climb rate. On flights as long as 500 miles it could comfortably carry the promised 2,000-pound payload in its cavernous, boxy cabin that had almost three times the cabin volume of the stock Beaver. On shorter runs, which most Otters flew, it could manage as much as 3,000 pounds. The seaplane version got off the water as quickly as the Beaver and could haul 2,000 pounds over 400 miles. In high-density seating, it could carry as many as 16 passengers, more than any other bushplane in service at the time.

The DHC-3 Otter was de Havilland's follow-up to the hugely successful Beaver. It was a larger aircraft with a sophisticated wing capable of lifting twice the Beaver's half-ton payload. It was a bit underpowered compared to the Beaver, but its wing largely compensated for this shortcoming.

Providing crucial support for forest firefighting was a key task for many Canadian Beavers, which flew teams of firefighters and their equipment into the field. Here water pumps flown in by Beavers are being set up and hoses are being run to fight a fire.

The Otter had some weaknesses too. On floats it could be a handful in a crosswind with the big rudder that was enlarged during flight tests to give it better ground control on wheels. For the lack of a little extra horsepower, the Otter's sustained climb rate at gross weight tapered off to not particularly impressive levels after the initial climb, especially in warm weather. Other than that, its only real weakness, which became apparent over time, was the durability of its engine when subjected to the beating the airplane took in intensive, short-haul bush use. The strain of frequent maximum performance take-offs with a bush operator's idea of a maximum load and the rapid and large engine temperature fluctuations encountered in the many ups and

The Beaver competed against the Fairchild Husky for the all-important first big order, which came from OPAS. The Husky, seen here, was larger and could carry a bigger load; but it was underpowered and had a less sophisticated wing, which resulted in poor STOL performance. Only 11 Huskies were built, but some were refitted with more powerful engines and flew for many years.

downs of a typical day's work slowly took their toll. The Otter eventually acquired a reputation for having a maintenance-intensive engine, which was expensive, and it experienced a higher (but by no means unacceptable) rate of engine failures than the Beaver.

Its more immediate drawback for the perpetually financially strapped bush operators was that a new Otter was prohibitively expensive for many of them and cost a lot more than a war-surplus

The bush division of Wien Alaska Airlines was a big operator of Beavers. One is seen here in new livery after Wien's merger with Northern Consolidated Airlines in the 1960s.

Norseman. Thus, out of 466 Otters built, only 107 were bought new by civilian operators. The rest went to various armed forces, including 69 to the Royal Canadian Air Force and 208 to the U.S. armed forces. The rest of the civilian world had to wait for the military Otters to be surplussed to afford to enjoy the benefits of the big bushplane.

Of the U.S. military Otters, 190 were bought by the Army after a competitive demonstration when DHC managed to get an Otter to participate in a major U.S. Army helicopter load-hauling exercise. The Otter, a modest sideshow at the exercise, hauled five times the load into the same battlefield environment at less cost than the most productive of the Army's H-21 Flying Bananas in the early, preturbine helicopter days.

The Otter's first operator in western Canada was Max Ward, who later became a national legend for his creation of Wardair and for his fierce battles with the Canadian bureaucracy along the way. At the time of the Otter's introduction, he was just another brash young bush pilot with a Fox Moth and an obsessive drive to succeed in aviation. Ward was a former Royal Canadian Air Force pilot who was found to be too good to be sent to the front and was kept at home to give flight instructions. He struggled to survive in the late 1940s as a one-man flying service with the Fox Moth out of Yellowknife to service the mines and a new government hydroelectric project on the Snare River, but he went out of business in 1949, foiled by the lowly capabilities of his airplane that couldn't earn him a living wage.

When Ward got wind of the Otter, he thought it might be time to get back into the bush-flying business and headed to DHC in Toronto to check it out. He had the demo flight of his life, which made him desperate for an Otter. As he recalled in his memoirs, *The Max Ward Story: A Bush Pilot in the Bureaucratic Jungle*, he strapped into the Otter, faced DHC's massive hangar, and expected to taxi out for takeoff after the usual ritual of firing up the airplane and getting organized for departure. Instead, George Neal, DHC's chief test pilot, firewalled the throttle and the Otter shot across the tarmac at the looming hangar. Just when Ward thought they were going to crash, the STOL wing went into action and the earth effortlessly fell away.

The Beaver has many tailor-made features for the convenience of the pilots and ground staff. Among the most popular is the waist-level refueling port. The Beaver has only belly tanks, which eliminates the uncomfortable and dangerous need to climb on top of the wings for refueling.

These skis, which retracted flush with the wing when the gear was raised, were especially designed for the Beech 18. The design looked promising, but proved to be too cumbersome and wasn't a success.

Making skis for aircraft is a niche business performed by specialist companies. When skis with retractable wheels were perfected in the early 1950s, they were so convenient that they replaced regular skis.

Max Ward received the fifth Otter off the production line, financed in part by a subsidized Canadian government business development program and in part by the mine for which he was going to do much of his flying. He had Wardair painted on its side and never looked back. His timing was right as mining activity was on the increase during the mid-1950s, including a boom in uranium mining. A Beaver joined Wardair's Otter, and within a few years, an Otter fleet of five aircraft and a mixed bag of others had a thriving business throughout the Northwest and Max Ward turned his attention to building his conventional airline business.

In Max Ward's view, one feature of the Otter brought a significant change in the standard of living in the Canadian bush. It was the first mass-produced bushplane that could carry the stock 4x8-foot plywood sheets that are the staple wallboard in construction throughout North America. With the arrival of the Otter, these sheets could be economically and easily flown into the smallest isolated settlements and mining camps, making affordable the construction of proper buildings on a large scale throughout the wilderness for the first time.

Ward's chief pilot, Don Braun, became one of the Otter's biggest fans. In his opinion, no aircraft compared to it in across-the-board performance, but he most valued its short field performance and load bearing, especially its ability to carry awkward, external loads. He routinely carried two 16-foot canoes, one strapped to each side, or a 26-foot freighter canoe on Wardair's Otters. He once strapped an entire Cessna 180 wing to the airplane's side. His most unusual external cargo was a 1,500-pound upright piano he flew into a mining community for a schoolteacher. Contrary to some Otter pilots, including DHC's chief test pilot, Braun never alluded to any issues with the Otter's climb rate fully loaded.

Braun loved the Otters, but Ward had bigger plans for him and Wardair, even in the bush. After he saw the larger scale mining operations in the North, Ward recognized the opportunity to fly cargo with a much bigger airplane and bought a Bristol Freighter powered by two 1,980-horsepower Hercules engines. It was a weird and wonderful tail-dragger with a big, bulbous nose that opened up to accommodate Caterpillar bulldozers of respectable size and similar equipment. In more genteel surroundings, it attracted notice as an aerial cross-channel car ferry between England and France.

Braun flew the big freighter for 12 years and landed it on the tundra and along lakeshores all over the northern wilderness wherever the oil and mining companies wanted their heavy equipment and supplies. The culmination of Braun's career flying Bristol was landing it at the North Pole in the summer of 1967 with an annual scientific polar expedition. It was the first wheeled aircraft to accomplish the feat.

Boffa and Phipps

Bush flying hummed in Canada during the 1950s and 1960s. Among the many bush pilots who became Canadian household words during this time were Ernie Boffa and Weldy Phipps. Boffa was one of the most experienced bush pilots at Canadian Pacific Airlines as its president, Grant McConachie, made it a major international airline to serve the Pacific to Australia with four-engine propliners. The company's first jets soon followed.

Boffa became a pilot in Montana in 1928 and barnstormed for years in the United States and Canada. He was an instructor in the RCAF during the war and joined Canadian Pacific in Yellowknife in 1943, initially to service the Eldorado uranium mine and several other mines flying in his Norseman. Boffa earned his reputation by being utterly reliable and exercising unfailing judgment. He accumulated superb knowledge of the vast terrain he covered and had an uncanny sense for navigation. He was as good a mechanic as a pilot and excelled at field repairs. It all added up to making the hard, uncertain slog of the bush pilot's daily routine appear to be as matter-of-fact as any normal airline run when he was flying.

Boffa achieved relative certainty on his daily routes in part by landing on any suitable patch in the wilderness when the weather was no longer flyable, waiting out the bad spell, and continuing on his way. He rarely turned back, but never continued into deteriorating conditions beyond reason. He always made the best

A Beaver in northern Canada drops off a party of geologists on a prospecting trip. The aircraft will keep the party supplied and retrieve them when their task is completed.

In addition to a spacious interior and cargo doors designed specifically to fit standard-sized fuel drums, the Beaver is prized for its ability to haul an external load. This Beaver is carrying building materials, a common external cargo in the bush.

CANADIAN
AVIATION
FIRST IN CANADA — 27th YEAR OF PUBLICATION

September, 19
25c

CF-GSK

Pacific Western Norseman prepares for a British Columbia flight.
SURVEY OF WESTERN AND NORTHERN BUSINESS FLYING (see page 38)
LET'S GO ON A BUSH FLIGHT (see page 40)
Complete Editorial Index on Page 3

While the Beaver and its larger stable mate, the Otter, received most of the attention in the mid-1950s, the Noorduyn Norseman kept on trucking. It was available in large numbers for a low price as war surplus aircraft and was an attractive option.

of these enforced interruptions for his passengers and often set up tents for them, devised ways to keep them occupied, and was occasionally trounced at cards by a jolly traveling priest who had been a professional magician in Europe before turning to the cloth and the Canadian Far North.

Boffa flew every type of bush trip out of Yellowknife in a variety of airplanes. He took prospectors to secret claims and circuit judges on their rounds. He flew search-and-rescue missions looking for missing prospectors deep in the dreaded Barrens. He made medical emergency flights, and mining and community resupply and mail flights. He took trappers and their sled dogs to their grounds and scientists on research projects. Every Christmas he flew the mission most popular with the communities he served and made his rounds with Santa Claus.

As Canadian Pacific turned into an international airline during the 1950s on routes Trans Canada Air Lines didn't want, Grant McConachie recognized it was time to start selling off the bush routes. Boffa was welcome to make the transition with Canadian Pacific into the left seat of a four-engine airliner, but he preferred to remain in the bush. McConachie, the consummate wheeler-dealer, understood and went out of his way to help. He heard that the Northern Construction Company, the contractor to build the DEW Line, needed an experienced Arctic pilot to locate and support the selected radar sites, and arranged for Boffa to get the job and fly a Canadian Pacific Norseman. Boffa worked on the DEW Line for three years and went on to roam the north as a contract pilot, enabled by his experience to pick the jobs he liked.

Another famed Canadian bush pilot and mechanic, Weldy Phipps, was a consummate innovator who modified aircraft to meet any unusual need throughout his long career. One intriguing project was his modification of war surplus F-5 Lightnings (the photo reconnaissance version of the P-38

A Beaver splashes down on an Alaskan lake more than 50 years after the first Beaver took flight.

fighter) for civilian high-altitude photo mapping work over large sections of Canada's remote regions. Phipps is best remembered for a simple, ingenious innovation that is still a fixture of bush flying today, the tundra tire.

Wheeled aircraft operating off-airport in the Arctic were restricted by the summer thaw. When the permafrost became sufficiently soft, the aircraft were bogged down and that was the end of flying for off-airport operations until the next freeze. Phipps was determined to find a way to extend the flying season because the alternative to continue working, the helicopter, was too expensive. He was prompted into action by a contract his company was trying to complete for the Geological Survey of Canada in the Arctic in the late 1950s.

Phipps noticed that the airplanes sank into the permafrost more readily than he did. He compared the soles of his boots relative to his weight with the tire surface supporting the Beavers and confirmed that the airplanes' weight needed to be better distributed. Phipps put oversized tires on a Super Cub and the results were what he had hoped for. Next, DC-3 tires were installed on a Beaver, with the ply partially shaved off to save weight and barely enough pressure in the tire to keep it round, and that worked too. Today a variety of tundra tires are offered by the tire manufacturers.

Fighting Fires

Water bombing forest fires was another important innovation that offered a new career niche for bush pilots and began in the 1950s under the auspices of the Ontario Provincial Air Service. OPAS had been experimenting with tossing out bags of water onto forest fires from its aircraft with unsatisfactory results and switched to investigating the possibilities of jettisoning large amounts of water from onboard water tanks.

The bush pilots held in highest regard were the ones who were also good mechanics and could tackle any mechanical problem in the field. Many of the early bush pilots started out as mechanics and became pilots after they perfected their first profession.

In the 1950s, wildlife management included the aerial culling of wolves, which were seen merely as pests, and the airplane provided game wardens the reach they needed. A Beaver from OPAS in Ontario, Canada, is seen here on wolf patrol.

Max Ward, founder of Wardair, was one of the first operators of the Otter. He received serial number 5 off the assembly line. Here he is seen right after World War II in his first aircraft, a Fox Moth. His difficulties with making a living with the obsolete Moth prompted his eager interest in the Otter.

The Otter was equally at home on wheels, skis, and floats. Many were equipped with the appropriate option, depending on the season.

The organization came up with a long, cylindrical tank inside a sleeve that could be mounted lengthwise on a float. Triggered by a mechanical release, the cylinder would rotate along its length and dump the water in one big, concentrated salvo. It was mounted on each float of a Beaver and produced promising results. A single airplane's water load was negligible, but a whole squadron could make a difference before a fire got out of hand. The Beavers were all equipped with the cylinders, and OPAS expressed an interest in the Otter because it needed an airplane to carry a bigger water load. From these beginnings OPAS and its successor, the Ontario Ministry of Natural Resources, built the formidable water bomber force that today flies the large multi-engined turboprop amphibian CL-415 made by Bombardier Aerospace. These unique aircraft can skim a lake and scoop up 1,200 gallons of water in six seconds. The load of water they carry weighs as much as two and a half fully loaded Beavers and is dropped in less than two seconds.

OPAS continued to do much of its flying the traditional way (floats in the summer, skis in the winter) and surveyed forests, tracked wildlife, managed the fish stock, and patrolled for forest fires, fighting them when they broke out. By the end of the 1950s and during the 1960s, a transformation slowly took place in bush flying throughout Canada and Alaska.

Hard-surface runways became widespread and encroached into the domain of the floatplane, which was beginning to give way to more efficient, faster, wheeled aircraft. Pilots across the board took advantage of an expanding network of navigation aids. On many routes bush flying was becoming more like normal commuter flying. By the 1970s, the floatplane was being challenged even in the southeast of Alaska by the appearance of hard-surface runways at Petersburg, Wrangell, Sitka, Haines, and Skagway.

A New Breed of Clients

The consolidation of air services continued, and in 1962, Alaska Coastal Airlines and Ellis Air Transport merged. Five years later, the new company was acquired by Alaska Airlines. The amphibians

Many Otters continue to fly the bush, but spare parts and rising maintenance demands are a problem, especially on the 600-horsepower Pratt and Whitney engine, which is not as widely available as the Beaver's smaller engine. The best solution is to convert the Beaver to a more modern Pratt and Whitney, a PT6 turboprop.

Max Ward observed that the Otter's ability to carry 4x8-foot plywood sheets, a mainstay of construction, profoundly changed lives by bringing affordable, easy-to-construct mainstream housing to the small, scattered settlements deep in the wilderness. This Alaskan Otter still carries the standard plywood sheets for constructing remote lodges.

An Otter is the star attraction in a timeless scene on an Alaskan waterway.

125

In spite of the Otter's modern technology, field conditions remained just as rough as in the H boat days. When a field change of a failed engine was required, the procedures were just the same as in the old days: hack a tripod out of nearby trees for engine support and go to it.

A U.S. Fish and Wildlife Service Super Cub departs on another wildlife survey flight. Note the extra window in the back for better observation. The L-4 military Cubs used for observation had similar aft windows.

OPAS was a pioneer of water bombing to fight forest fires. The Beaver was the first aircraft with an operational capability to deliver a salvo of water. The aircraft fast taxied to force water into the tanks mounted on its floats. It dumped its load by rotating the cylinders lengthwise into the open position. One Beaver made little difference, but a squadron of them bombing in quick succession could prevent small fires from getting out of hand.

were around for a few more years, but Alaska Airlines' primary interest was linking the southeast's two main destinations, Juneau and Ketchikan, with the rest of the state and the outside world. In time it was content to leave most of the local routes to smaller operators. In 1968, Alaska Airlines acquired Cordova Airlines along with Mudhole Smith as an executive. But given Alaska Airlines' lack of interest in feeder services, Smith managed to retain Cordova's bush division for himself and served the local communities that had long been his main source of livelihood.

Except for a few diehards and authentic eccentrics of the bush, most locals felt their quality of life improved as the air services were able to take passengers in stock commuter aircraft and airliners to proper airports just like air services anywhere else. But as the role of the true bush pilot appeared to be on the wane, an interesting phenomenon occurred. There had always been a steady trickle of well-heeled sportsmen visiting Alaska, but now passengers with money to spend began to show up in huge numbers and demanded to be flown deep into the wilderness. They were looking for escape from hard-surface runways, airport lounges, and their normal lives. They wanted to be flown into lakeside cabins, dropped off at isolated hunting cabins, land on glaciers, and taken to see the ice caps, and they gave traditional bush flying a new lease on life.

The first big OPAS water bomber was the Catalina amphibian, or the Canso. It adopted the mechanisms perfected on the Beaver and Otter and was the first water bomber that could dump an effective load.

The turboprop Canadair CL-415 is the ultimate water bomber. It is the culmination of decades of experience that goes back to experiments with the Norseman and the Beaver in the 1940s. A CL-415 can scoop up 1,200 gallons of water, the weight of two and a half fully loaded Beavers, in six seconds and dump it even faster.

Mt. McKinley in Alaska's Denali National Park provides the backdrop for one of the state's most prolific professional photographers. Mac flew his own Piper Cub to field assignments during the 1950s and 1960s.

Fat tundra tires on this Piper Super Cub spread its weight around by burdening the ground with less weight per square inch of tire surface than smaller tires, enabling airplanes to operate off softer ground.

The Cessna 185 is one of the most successful bushplanes in the category just below the Beaver. In addition to being able to haul a good load and deliver good takeoff and landing performance, it is also faster than many piston-powered bushplanes.

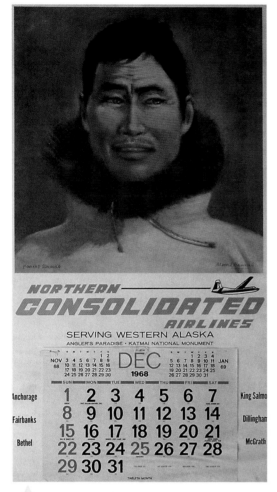

This rare calendar dates from the last days of Northern Consolidated Airways, which was formed by the merger of several small outfits including Petersen Air Service and Jim Dodson Air Service. By the end of the year it merged with Wien Air. The new company was called Wien Consolidated Airlines.

The Swiss Pilatus Porter was an excellent but expensive bushplane that was well liked by Wien Air and the CIA.

A Wien Air Boeing 737 touches down at Prudhoe Bay. This aircraft is miles away from the Standard biplanes Noel Wien used at the beginning of his bush-flying career, but the gravel runway under its wheels is an unmistakable reminder of the airline's roots.

Chapter 5

A Turbine Otter and three Cessna 185s from K2 Aviation await the day's missions at Talkeetna, the main airport for flights around Mt. McKinley and the Denali region. Note the hydraulically retractable skis on the aircraft. The Otter is parked overnight with the skis down for greater stability. During the winter, K2's Turbine Otters do seismic work for the oil companies in the Arctic, based at Deadhorse in the Prudhoe Bay region.

Still by the Seat
of Their Pants

On a windswept, rainy summer day at Juneau Airport, Alaska Airlines' Boeing 737s nose up to the jetways. Passengers while away their time and wait for their flights at generic, nondescript twenty-first-century airport gates. Those who are inclined to be more observant may be startled to see an airplane that looks like an antique taxi by the windows. It is a brawny, radial-engined white and maroon de Havilland Otter on huge amphibious floats. It is not an antique on its way to an airshow. It is Wings Airways Flight 75, the midday flight to the small Tinglit island settlements of Angoon and Tenakee Springs. Seventy years after floatplanes showed up in southeast Alaska, the only way to fly to these destinations is still by floatplane flown by the seat of the pants.

Hard-surface runways in a number of larger communities in southeast Alaska have reduced the role of the floatplane, but many of the smaller communities along the coastal island system are still reachable only on floats (helicopters are still a prohibitively expensive alternative). Small armadas of floatplanes and amphibians operated by a handful of air services shuttle a mix of local residents, outside visitors, and cargo to these communities from the larger towns of Ketchikan, Sitka, and Juneau on scheduled and nonscheduled runs. While air services like Wings of Alaska serve many of their scheduled destinations with aircraft on wheels, the rhythm and character of the region's daily floatplane operations differ little from the time of Ellis Air Transport and Alaska Coastal Airlines.

Floatplanes also remain a fixture in the southeast on a seasonal basis because of a much bigger market brought every year by the endless summer parade of cruise ships up and down the Inland Passage. Cruise ships took 1.6 million passengers on Alaskan cruises in 2003. At the various stops that take up most days of a typical cruise, thousands of passengers sign up to be stunned by the scenery from the air and taste a bit of the sensation of being set down in pristine wilderness not easily reached by other means.

Wings of Alaska has a separate operation, Wings Airways, dedicated entirely to the cruise ship business. Its fleet of three Beavers and four Otters fly from the old Alaska Coastal Airlines jetties on the downtown Juneau waterfront right next to where the cruise ships dock.

According to Mike Stedman, chief pilot for Wings of Alaska and Wings Airways, 25,000 cruise passengers were flown by the floatplanes from the Juneau docks in 2003. Stedman is the nephew of Bill Stedman, retired Alaska Coastal and Alaska Island Airways Goose pilot. Inspired by his uncle, Stedman, a second-generation Alaskan, has been a professional pilot since age 20. He spent the first nine years of his flying career as a fish spotter for commercial fishing boats.

Stedman is a hands-on chief pilot and is often at the controls on both the scheduled flights and the floatplane tours from the docks. The floatplane tours fly two types of missions,

Wings of Alaska's Otter has amphibious floats and takes passengers where no jetliner can go, half a century after the type's introduction. This Otter is departing Juneau on an early morning run to Angoon and Tenakee Springs.

the Juneau ice cap flights and a flight to Taku Lodge. What was once a regular stop on Frank Barr's beat between Atlin and Juneau is now a fly-in tour destination. Taku Lodge is owned today by another Alaskan bush pilot, Ken Ward, whose own fleet of aircraft also keeps the visitors coming.

A Look at the Early Days

It is unlikely that many passengers on the ice cap flights in the floatplanes realize how authentic a glimpse they get of a certain aspect of bush flying from the early days. The old Vegas, Stinsons, Fairchilds, and other aircraft out of Juneau bound for points in Canada in the 1930s and 1940s departed across the ice cap in good weather along the same route to head for their destinations across the blinding ice and ragged, austere peaks. Slowly droning above the vast Juneau Ice Field with half a dozen glaciers in view at once, it is sobering to think of how utterly alone and exposed a pilot was in the pre-radio days in case of a forced landing.

While tens of thousands of passengers are hauled above the glaciers today, ice cap tours have been a staple of the bush pilot's repertoire from the earliest days. The day after Anscel Eckmann and Bob Ellis arrived in Juneau in 1929 to establish Alaska-Washington Airways, the southeast's first sustained air service, they were hauling fare-paying passengers in their Vega over the Juneau Ice Cap. On one good day they made more than $1,000, which was a fortune in those days.

Today, Juneau's floatplanes vie with swarms of helicopters for the cruise passenger glacier tour business. The helicopter can profitably charge a price passengers are willing to pay and offer glacier landings, but the fixed-wing crowd can hold its own against the helicopters because they can show their passengers the same scenery for half the price. A surprising number of passengers want to fly a floatplane for its nostalgic link to the past or its sheer romance.

Another major source of business for modern-day bush services are the millions of visitors who come to Alaska annually for fishing, hunting, or nature and eco trips. They need transportation into the pristine wilderness, and for many of them, a bushplane is still the only way to go. Wings' business is rounded out by charter work and flown mostly by a Cessna 206 amphibian or the Beavers. Most charters are to lodges and fishing cabins and to drop off people on bear viewing trips to Admiralty Island, home to Alaska's biggest brown bears.

This takeoff is under visual flight rules, Alaska style. Special clearance is used to depart controlled airports, and in the state's vast tracts of uncontrolled airspace, 1-mile visibility and staying clear of clouds is the legal norm for flying visually.

Cargo and passengers share the Otter's utilitarian cabin. Carrying the mail is also still an important role for many bush operators.

One of the Otter's best-liked features is the individual door on each side of the cockpit, which frees the pilots from scrambling over cargo. It is a feature that first appeared on the Noorduyn Norseman, the first purpose-designed bushplane.

"Whatever the job, action is based on the equipment I have to work with and the preservation of that equipment. For while it is intact, you are all right, but when you wreck a pontoon or the whole plane, you are out of business."

—Shell Simmons

The story is much the same throughout the southeast. Ketchikan is the busiest floatplane base in the region. The fleets of Beavers, Turbine Otters, and Cessnas lining the Ketchikan waterfront come and go nonstop from dawn to dusk on tours, scheduled runs, and charters. When bad weather closes in, they don't stop much before the seagulls call it a day. Aside from regular transportation to nearby island stops, Misty Fjord National Park is the big attraction here.

The midday flight from Juneau arrives at the settlement of Angoon on Admiralty Island. The big amphibian is Angoon's quickest link to the outside world.

Floatplanes can still be found on the Sitka waterfront, and helicopters have the lion's share of the glacier tour business in Skagway. There are hundreds of privately owned floatplanes throughout the region, including Piper Cubs, Aeroncas, a whole range of Cessnas, and even the occasional Beaver. The drone of the Grumman Goose is no longer heard in this part of Alaska, but a few still fly the island routes farther south along the Canadian coast.

Private Bushplanes

Private floatplanes are such an essential and everyday way of getting around the southeast's great outdoors that many don't change hands for decades. Don Bedford, who started working for Alaska Coastal Airlines in Juneau in 1947 and retired from Alaska Airlines nearly four decades later, bought his Taylorcraft in 1948 and flew it long into retirement. He kept it at Auk Lake, across the street from his home, where it was parked as casually as a car. He called it *No Got* for no got starter, no got generator, and no got lights.

A consummate fisherman and hunter, Bedford used the airplane for his pastimes and to fly to the family's lakeshore summer cabin. For years he worked the night shift at the airline so he could fly during part of the day. He never worried about the weather much and followed the simple rule of flying until you can land ahead on suitable water and making a U-turn before you need to land.

The day's catch came home in the Taylorcraft's floats with a little water thrown in to keep things fresh. He'd give the local kids a fish or two out of the floats back home on Auk Lake to play with until the long bureaucratic pole of the fish warden caught up with him and accused him of illegally stocking Auk Lake. At age 81 Bedford is still adamant that he'd never own an airplane on wheels.

One item of aviation gear Bedford never owned that has made life simpler and safer for bush pilots everywhere since the 1990s is a global positioning system (GPS). These inexpensive, accurate navigation units, equipped with moving map displays and driven by information beamed down from satellites, have made navigation infinitely easier in the bush. While they have undeniably reduced some of the challenge by taking the tension and potential uncertainty out of navigation in poor

Following a quick stop, Angoon recedes behind the Otter's floats. The floatplane dock is in the small bay in the upper left corner, to the left of the settlement.

137

African Affair

Africa has been one of the most romanticized environments for bush flying ever since Dennis Finch Hatton and Beryl Markham started spotting game for safaris in their tiny, resilient Cirrus Moths during the 1930s. African flying was pioneered by a series of highly publicized survey and record flights running the length of the continent from various European points of departure in the 1920s and 1930s. The airplane quickly established itself in every conceivable manifestation of its many bush roles in every corner of Africa. Its role in wildlife management, tourism, and humanitarian support is still poignant.

Bush flying also fulfills other traditional tasks, such as supporting companies engaged in natural resource extraction, such as mining, oil exploration and production, and logging. The well-capitalized mining and oil companies usually have networks of well-graded private airfields, many of them hard surfaced, and large fleets of expensive turbine helicopters. Companies on smaller budgets, such as the loggers of West Africa working deep in the forests, often still hack a rough dirt strip out of the jungle for the aircraft that are their lifeline to the outside. A typical bush service that supported them was Avia Service of Douala, Cameroon, that flew for the logging camps on a compass and clock in the Congo Basin through the 1980s.

For months at a time, the only connection to the outside world for these loggers in Africa is the airplane.

The Kika airstrip on the Ngoka River in West Africa is not the customary environment of a Piper Cheyenne turboprop.

Most of Avia's destinations were not found on any air navigation map, and the maps covering sections of their area still carry the warning "Maximum elevation figures are believed not to exceed 4,600 feet" and "Incomplete." Avia's mixed bag of Piper Cheyenne and T-1040 turboprops and various piston aircraft left Douala's modern international airport, tracked a succession of two VORs on course until they lost the last one, and then they were on their own for the last 280 miles or so in the days before GPS. Mostly they flew by compass and clock in this wettest part of Africa where even on a good day there are often layers of clouds from close to the ground to well above 20,000 feet. Position reporting was on HF radio to Brazzaville, far to the south.

The pilots employed an old navigation technique to get the dead reckoning right in an environment of unknown winds. They were typically heading for a camp on a sizable river, so they deliberately offset their course to the north of the camp by 5 to 10 degrees to know which way to turn when they found the river. When approaching the river in cloud, they descended about half an hour ahead of their estimated arrival time to be sure not to cross it. They had conservative descent limits in a general area where they were sure of the maximum elevations and if they didn't break out of cloud by the expected altitude, they climbed and went home. If they saw ground, they kept going until the river showed up and they followed it to their first stop. On most flights they called on several camps before heading home. The logs their clients were floating downriver would take eight months to make the 1,000-mile journey to the sea, the only other way out of the camps.

Mishaps were rare, but they did occur. One pilot's compass was inadvertently affected by the magnetic effect of a heavy generator he was carrying in a Cherokee. He became hopelessly disoriented and disappeared. Three weeks after he was given up for lost, he showed up at a camp; he had been guided out of the forest by local pygmies.

An aircraft circles the Bela logging camp to signal its arrival. The logs take eight months to make their way on the river to the Atlantic ports for on-shipment.

weather, they haven't lessened the need for the pilots' skills required to handle the airplane safely in its unique environment, nail the interpretation of the weather every time, and get the flight planning right. Bush pilots who last in the business soon know their territory like the back of their hands and can get around in it as easily as someone driving to the local supermarket or to work.

Don Bedford finally stored the old Taylorcraft, but his son plans to put it back in the water as soon as he finds enough time away from his job at Alaska Airways.

Flying Tourists

Beyond the southeast's traditional floatplane services for the local community, Alaskan bush flying remains closest to its roots as it serves the

"It's sharpening my wits. I want to keep sharpening my wits."

—Bob Reeve

Flying low and slow and gluing a wingtip to the coastline has been a bush pilot tactic in poor weather from the earliest days. When the weather turns unflyable en route, floatplanes often land and taxi on water the rest of the way to their destination.

139

The huge Juneau ice cap towers right over the town, but few local residents ever really saw it until the airplane arrived. Locals were enthusiastic flightseers from the day in 1929 when Anscel Eckmann showed up in his Lockheed Vega and started selling rides.

tourist industry. Sport fishermen and hunters had always been an important niche business for bush pilots. But as spending power increased and the airlines brought Alaska within easy, affordable reach, Ray Petersen was one of the first Alaskan aviators to see the full potential of tourism to become a main source of revenue for bush-flying services. Petersen had been was the driving force behind the consolidation of several bush lines into Northern Consolidated Airways.

In 1950, Petersen accurately foresaw the long-term boom in tourism that was then just beginning. With the fierce competition among the small bush services before the big consolidations, he saw that passively waiting for the tourists to arrive and fighting it out with innumerable charter services would be marginally profitable for all concerned. The solution was for the bush service that flew tourists to a lodge or fishing camp to own the facility. Or, alternatively, for a lodge or camp business to own its own bush-flying outfit. Then the all-inclusive price of a stay would include the bush flights and the bush operator would have a captive, sustainable business.

Petersen worked with Alaska state tourism officials and established three fishing lodges owned by Northern Consolidated Airways in the Katmai National Park on the Katmai peninsula. The park covers 4.3 million acres, twice the size of Yellowstone National Park. It has 15 volcanoes within its boundaries, 8 major river systems, and one of the biggest concentrations of brown bears in the world. The fishing is some of the best on the planet. The Katmai offers rainbow and trout, arctic grayling, pike, and five types of salmon, including king and sockeye. During the season more than 100,000 sockeye salmon crowd the Nanek drainage system alone.

The flight from Anchorage is relatively short and runs along the old bush-flying run to King Salmon and the canneries on Bristol Bay. The two Angler's Paradise Fishing Lodges and Brooks Lodge established by Petersen became a family business as the airline world changed. They are now operated by his son and are

The terrain and challenge are little changed from the time this Fairchild made its way over the ice cap to Juneau.

among the most coveted fishing destinations in the state. Clients arrive by floatplane, which is still the only way to get to the lodges. The floatplanes are also available to fly the most insatiable guests to various fishing spots within a 100-mile radius during their stay.

A New Kind of Bush Pilot

As commuter-style flying took hold to most destinations within Alaska and bush flying thrived primarily in the tourism niche, an increasingly popular type of new bush pilot was the licensed fishing and hunting guide who was also a commercial pilot with his own airplane. Among them was Hank Rust, founder of Rust's Flying Service, which is one of the biggest Alaskan bush services today with float operations on Lake Hood and a wheeled fleet at Talkeetna that serves Mt. McKinley.

Rust joined the U.S. Army Air Force during World War II and flew B-25 bombers in New Guinea. His wartime service led to a 20-year Air Force career, with the last three years served in Alaska. When Rust, an avid outdoorsman, retired in 1963, he made the easy transition into a 180-horsepower Piper Super Cub and became the pilot-guide as owner and sole employee of Rust's Flying Service. Rust guided fishing trips during the summer, and led caribou, moose, and bear hunting expeditions during the fall and winter. He flew throughout the state, and even led polar bear hunts far out onto the Siberian ice cap. Clients flew via commercial airlines to Point Hope to join Rust and head out over the ice in the Super Cub.

Fly-in hunting trips became so popular and effective that they began to excessively stack the odds against the prey. So many hunters wanted to be landed next to their quarry, shoot it, and be back in town for cocktails that the authorities passed a regulation that required fly-in hunters to wait overnight before beginning the hunt.

As Rust's business thrived, he acquired his first fishing lodge in 1970. Today the company

Piper Super Cub

Year introduced: 1949
Engine: Lycoming O-320
Fuel: 36 gallons
Gross weight: 1,750 pounds
Payload (with full fuel): 429 pounds
Seats: 2
Cruise speed: 115 miles per hour
Highlights: The Super Cub is a small feisty hauler and an excellent STOL and high-altitude performer. It's preferred by guide pilots who do a lot of off-airfield landings with one or two customers.

In spite of modern developments, flying through mountain passes close to the ground still poses the same challenges confronted by bush pilots from earlier times.

Urban Bush Pilots

When most people hear the words *bush pilot*, they picture someone in a plaid shirt, baseball cap, jeans, and work boots, or imagine a defiant face gazing out of a bundle of fur in a biplane on ice in a black-and-white photo. There are bush pilots who fly in white dress shirts, black ties, and slacks, and the shadow that looms over their Beaver is often a skyscraper. They are the urban bush pilots who fly floatplanes from such coastal cities as Vancouver, British Columbia, and Seattle, Washington.

Being an urban bush pilot is a curious occupation because they connect major metropolitan centers with a maze of nearby islands that are too far for bridges and most quickly reached by floatplane. The choice is easy between a 20-minute flight and a 3-hour ferry ride.

Harbour Air of Vancouver flies its Beavers, Turbine Otters, and Cessna 185s from Canada Place right in the middle of the city's business district to a variety of nearby destinations, including their most frequent run to Victoria, British Columbia's provincial capital that is a short flight offshore on Vancouver Island. The company also performs mail runs to small island communities and does its share of tours and charter work to the islands and into the stunning Alpine mountains nearby. Pilots who can't choose between bush flying and city life don't have to decide. They can fly all day in bush country without having to move there.

Floatplanes are seen here at Canada Place on the Vancouver, British Columbia, waterfront.

he built is run by his son, Todd, and daughter-in-law, Suzanne, and has grown substantially. Todd grew up in the business but was an aeronautical engineer at Lockheed before he returned to fly for the family firm. Suzanne came north from Oklahoma for a summer season and decided to stay indefinitely. Rust's Flying Service has expanded and owns over a dozen private self-catering fishing camps scattered within floatplane striking distance from Lake Hood, where it is the biggest floatplane operator. Four Cessna 206s, four Beavers, and a Turbine Otter make up the floatplane fleet, and there is a Cherokee on wheels for errands to places with runways.

Anchorage's Lake Hood is still the largest floatplane base in the world. In the 1960s it was joined with Lake Spenard by parallel channels that provide a long water runway and taxiway. The lake is the best example of how all levels of aviation can coexist in a community where an airplane ranks on par with the family car. The floatplane base is part of Anchorage International Airport, one of the largest air cargo hubs of the United States. The runway system for the commercial airliners is across the airport road from the lake. Tourist-laden floatplanes and an incessant stream of Boeing 747 freighters hauling goods from the Far East coexist happily, and often land and depart on parallel tracks, but are kept apart by procedures and the skilled controllers. On the other side of the floatplane base is a general aviation runway for all the wheeled general aviation aircraft that find it more convenient to base out of here than downtown Merrill Field.

Successful bush-flying services are always on the lookout for possibilities to expand, and Rust's Flying Service had a major opportunity to grow in 1996. It doubled its size with the acquisition of Talkeetna-based K2 Aviation, the biggest operator specializing in servicing the 20,320-foot Mt. McKinley, the highest spot in North America, and the environment around it.

K2 provides scenic flights and charters to support mountain climbing parties with a fleet of four Cessna 185s, two Turbine Otters, and a Beaver. All these airplanes are equipped with retractable skis for glacier landings. In 2002, K2 landed 3,500 people on the glaciers of Mt. McKinley. The company also has a pressurized Piper Navajo commuter that is used for high-altitude scenic tours that take passengers above the 12,500-foot limit of the other aircraft and can circle just above the peak for some of the grandest views.

K2's busiest days are when the short climbing season is on and parties of climbers clamor to be flown to base camps on McKinley's glaciers without delay. By late summer, the climbing season is over for the year and the Turbine Otter and the other aircraft taxi out for their most common mission, a sightseeing flight around Mt. McKinley, topped off by a glacier landing before returning to Talkeetna.

The Turbine Otter's smoothly burbling Pratt & Whitney PT-6 turbine engine gives it STOL performance the airplane's designers could only dream of. In the PT-6 the Otter received the extra power it should have always had and turbine reliability to boot. But it is expensive to realize the Otter's full potential. At more than half a million dollars, the engine alone costs three times the price of an entire piston-powered Otter when it was factory new.

The Turbine Otters are conversions carried out by firms specializing in aircraft modifications for niche markets. In spite of the price tag of around three quarters of a million dollars for a fully refurbished, converted Otter, the economics make sense for high-volume operators because the alternative best suited for the Turbine Otter's missions, a new Cessna Caravan with the same engine and payload capacity, costs around $3 million.

"Experience is something you get 10 minutes after you need it."

—Harvey Hobbs

Cessna 185

Year introduced: 1961
Engine: 260-horsepower Continental IO-470
Fuel: 84 gallons
Gross weight: 3,200 pounds
Payload (with full fuel): 950 pounds
Seats: 6
Cruise speed: 130 miles per hour
Highlights: The best of the smaller Cessnas, the 185 was fast, powerful, and a good load for its size. Later models had 300-horsepower engines. Many are still in service on floats, wheels, and skis.

Routine Glacier Flights

Flights around Mt. McKinley and glacier landings have been a mainstream business for at least the last three decades, flown by outfits based in Talkeetna. The landing spots used on the glaciers today and the procedures for flying in and out of them are so well established that for experienced pilots, the flights are routine. The ability to fly the mountain was hard earned, mostly by Don Sheldon, one of the last bush pilots whose story is told in one of the great classics on bush flying, *Wager the Wind* by James Greiner.

Don Sheldon received global publicity when *Life* magazine featured his daring mountain rescue flights in the 1960s, but by then he was long established as the man to see for flights to Mt. McKinley.

Sheldon experimented with landing on Mt. McKinley in 1951 when retractable skis became available. Equipping his Super Cub with a pair of the new skis, he picked up where Joe Crosson had left off in 1932. There had been flights on McKinley since Crosson's first flights, but never on a sustained basis. Sheldon taught himself to read the glaciers with great care and paid obsessive attention to the mechanical condition of his aircraft. He found an ideal aircraft with great STOL performance and the ability to climb well at high altitude in the Piper Super Cub with a 150-horsepower engine.

The main opportunity for Sheldon to start serious mountain flying was a need by Bradford Washburn, a scientist, mountaineer, and later director of Boston's Museum of Science, for a permanent pilot to support his long-term mapping project of Mt. McKinley. It was the start of a friendship like the one Washburn developed with Bob Reeve (Sheldon's father-in-law) in the 1930s when the pair flew together out of Valdez during Washburn's mountaineering expeditions in that region.

As Sheldon gained experience flying McKinley, he established regular landing spots on the glaciers near ideal base camp locations for climbing the mountain. This was the beginning of the business of flying mountaineers and their supplies to the mountain, which saved them days of trekking in and out and the expenses of pack trains that added up to considerably more than the cost of the

Regardless of a flight's purpose in Alaska or Canada, many trips are an impromptu geology lesson in glacier structure.

Cessna 208 Caravan

Year introduced: 1982
Engine: 675-horsepower Pratt and Whitney Canada PT6-A
Fuel: 335 gallons
Gross weight: 8,000 pounds
Payload (with full fuel): 2,200 pounds
Seats: 12
Cruise speed: 176 miles per hour
Highlights: An excellent bush turboprop, and in bushplane terms a relatively new design, but at almost $3 million it is too expensive for most operators.

flights. For most of the mountain flights, Sheldon used the bigger Cessna 180s with their greater load-bearing ability, which he bought unpainted to save the 30-pound weight of the paint. But for pure performance, he always favored the more agile Super Cub.

Sheldon's regular bush-flying business continued to flourish, and a few years after he met Washburn, he made one of the most daring rescues of his career. Flying a two-passenger Aeronca on floats, he endangered himself to rescue eight Army surveyors, in as many flights, from a stretch of raging rapids in the Devil's Canyon on the Susitna River. Following a difficult landing through the narrow canyon, he coolly "ran" the rapids with his floatplane for each of seven pickups, and floated through them farther downriver to a stretch of smooth water for each takeoff. Then he returned to retrieve the eighth soldier farther downstream, who had been given up for lost by everyone else.

In addition to the routine glacier flights to often-climbed mountains, Sheldon took parties of climbers to any mountain of their choice and dropped them off and supported them at carefully researched landing sites suitably close to their destination. One of his most outstanding achievements, which received global media coverage, was the dramatic rescue of two parties of mountain climbers on Mt. McKinley. A party of four climbers was immobilized at 17,500 feet by a fall. Not much lower, a climber in another party was suffering from severe altitude sickness.

Following a radio call to the U.S. Air Force's rescue organization at Elmendorf Air Force Base in Anchorage, Sheldon was first on the scene with survival supplies. Dodging clouds and sucking supplemental oxygen, he rode his Super Cub to 19,000 feet and located the distressed climbers. When two Army helicopters floundered because of mechanical and navigation problems on the way to the site, Sheldon took charge and ferried five rescue teams to a spot at 10,000 feet.

He then received a radio call from the climbers that the climber with altitude sickness was comatose and wouldn't last much longer. Her companions could get her down to about 14,000 feet.

It's not hard to guess what the owner of this Harley-Davidson motorcycle does for a living. It belongs to Mike Stedman, chief pilot of Alaska Wings, and the Grumman Goose is one his Uncle Bill flew for years.

Cruise tours are big business for Wings Airways' hard-working Beavers and Otters.

The floatplane dock at Juneau looks much like it did in the days of Alaska Coastal Airlines. The basic dock pylon structure is original, but the old Alaska Coastal buildings were destroyed by fire and were replaced with the current structure. Floatplanes fly more than 25,000 passengers from this location on flightseeing recreational flights.

Sheldon decided to try and get her out with his Super Cub. As he was pondering his next move, he got a call from Washburn in Cambridge, Massachusetts, who had heard on the radio about the rescue in progress and knew McKinley better than anyone else. Sheldon was grateful for the call because in spite of his own great knowledge of the mountain, he needed the scientist's advice on a potential landing field. Washburn identified a shelf between two outcroppings of rock at 14,300 feet in the vicinity of the climbers and carefully described it to Sheldon, who departed without delay.

Accompanied by another Super Cub flown by experienced Anchorage-based bush pilot George Kitchen, Sheldon tackled the ice shelf specified by Washburn. It was just long enough. Kitchen came in second and got stuck in the snow that blocked the departure path. It took three hours to muscle his airplane out of the way, but Sheldon lunged down the shelf with the woman on board and had her down in Talkeetna within half an hour. She lived.

There were still the remaining climbers on a ledge at 17,500 feet where Sheldon couldn't go, and two of them were too injured to move. The tenacious bush pilot had a chance to work together with a helicopter, the craft that in coming years took over the mountain rescue business. The helicopter of the hour was a civilian two-place Hiller, huffing and puffing on a piston engine, flown up from Anchorage by Link Luckett of Hughes Helicopter Service.

The bobbling Hiller had a service ceiling of only 16,500 feet, but as it struggled upward, dwarfed by the mountain, Luckett, who had removed the heavy battery after starting the engine, coaxed the extra altitude out of the helicopter and plopped it down next to the stranded men. His altimeter read 17,230 feet, the highest any Hiller had ever been. He airlifted the two injured climbers to a shelf at 14,300 feet, one at a time, where Sheldon was waiting with the Super Cub. The two uninjured climbers made it there on foot and Sheldon flew all of them to the landing spot at 10,000 feet from where other aircraft completed the rescue. Sheldon made 18 round trips to Talkeetna to take the rescue parties off the mountain before he called it a day.

Don Sheldon died from cancer at an age when many of today's bush pilots start second careers flying Mt. McKinley during the summer season. The most popular landing spot he pioneered and where many pilots follow even today is known as the Sheldon Amphitheater. His business, Talkeetna Air Service, also lives on under a succession of new owners, who included Lowell Thomas Jr., one-time lieutenant governor of Alaska.

Some Jobs are Seasonal

Like a lot of bush pilots flying today, many of K2's and Rust's pilots come up for the climbing season. Many are retired or semiretired from earlier careers and are flexible with their time. One pilot, a former engineer from Livermore, California, runs his own aerobatic school in the off-season back home. The opportunities for earning a living full time year round as a bush pilot have diminished over the years. This is a problem not only for the pilots but also for the flying services. Todd and Suzanne Rust don't like having to haul their floatplanes out of the water in the fall and watch them sit on the beach for four to six months.

With soaring insurance costs, there is some pressure to find higher, less seasonal usage for the bush fleets. The Rusts have found a great winter niche for the Turbine Otters. They send them up north to Deadhorse. From there, the Otters do seismic work throughout the Prudhoe Bay region for the oil companies. Their task can only be done in the winter when the tundra is hard enough for the Otters to land. Rusts' has also found more permanent work out of Anchorage, flying power company workers to remote locations beyond the reach of the commuters, but visitors to the wilderness remain the core of the business.

Bush-flying services that perform jobs similar to Rust's Flying Service are scattered throughout Alaska. Many are based in Fairbanks, the state's other large regional hub besides Anchorage. Others await their clients at the end of the commuter lines, and air taxis run deeper in the wilderness. Some are one-person pilot-guide operations, and others fly a handful of aircraft; but all are available as in the old days to take their passengers to any stretch of water or turf that suits their purpose along the old bush routes into the Kuskokwim, along the Yukon, or into the Brooks Range and the rest of the Arctic.

Enduring in Canada

Half a continent away from the austere Brooks Range, on Ranger Lake in Ontario, Canada, a Beaver gently rocks on the water. A dirt logging road leads to the lake off the main highway from Sault Ste. Marie to Thunder Bay. North of here, the roads are still few and far between among the

The helicopter has made significant inroads into the traditional bushplane's tasks, but it is too expensive to buy and run compared to fixed-wing bushplanes.

Hard-surface airports, like this strip at Skagway, have made life easier for bush pilots, but according to some, they have taken the bush out of flying. The Cessna Caravan, introduced in the 1970s, is one of few bushplanes still being built and shares the ramp with a Piper Cherokee.

147

Fokker Super Universal

Year introduced: 1929
Engine: 410-horsepower Pratt & Whitney Wasp
Fuel: 125 gallons
Gross weight: 3,500 pounds
Payload (with full fuel): 600 pounds
Seats: 8
Cruise speed: 98 miles per hour
Highlights: More than 90 standard and Super Universals were built.
It was popular in the Canadian bush for its great STOL performance.
A long-term weakness was its wooden wing that was prone to wood rot.

de Havilland DHC-2 Turbine Beaver

Year introduced: 1963
Engine: 550-horsepower Pratt & Whitney Canada PT6A
Fuel: 95 gallons
Gross weight: 5,090 pounds
Payload (with full fuel): 1,157 pounds
Seats: 7
Cruise speed: 155 miles per hour
Highlights: It made an already excellent performer stellar but was too
expensive for the size of the airplane to attract a large market.

endless vista of forest and lakes that stretch over a thousand miles toward the Arctic. Punch Dickins wouldn't have far to fly in a Fokker Universal to feel at home. There are no roads to the best fishing lakes in the area, which is where the Beaver comes in.

The airplane is one of four owned by Air Dale, one of Canada's oldest bush services founded primarily to serve the fishing camps it owns. The Beaver has the local business to itself and serves five fishing camps on five different lakes in the vicinity. Air Dale's three other Beavers are based about 100 miles to the north on Hawk Lake near Wawa where they serve another 18 camps owned by Air Dale. One camp can accommodate as many as 24 guests, but most are smaller, and quite a few are the only camp on their lake. A handful take only four visitors and are available for even fewer guests who really want to get away from it all. When all 23 camps are full, they can accommodate 168 guests, quite a handful for a fleet of four Beavers.

Air Dale, a third-generation family business, was founded after World War II by Sonny and Laureen Dale. The couple was among the biggest fur buyers in Ontario going back to the 1930s. By the 1940s, Sonny Dale flew his own Fairchild KR-34 on floats during his fur-buying trips all over the province. By the end of World War II, the fur industry was in the doldrums and the couple looked for alternatives. With their flying skills, area knowledge, and good business sense, they saw an emerging opportunity in the fishing lodge business and bet on it with three lodges.

The KR-34 was supplanted by a growing fleet of SeaBees, which were suited for summer lodge work. The only drawback in Air Dale's use was the inability to attach external loads, such as canoes, to them. The six SeaBees later gave way to Cessnas, a Norseman, and a twin Beech. Beavers joined the fleet when Ontario's Ministry of Natural Resources put its older models on the market. Sonny Dale's fur-buying KR-34, which had originally belonged to OPAS (absorbed into the MNR), now hangs in the Canadian Bushplane Heritage Center in Sault Ste. Marie. Until a few years ago, Air Dale also had an Otter, but it was too expensive to maintain. The costly conversion to the turbine version made no economic sense for a company the size of Air Dale, so the Beavers pull the full load and do an excellent job.

Resurrection

The big problem with the DHC-2 Beaver is that it isn't being manufactured today. A group of investors have announced their intention to restart Beaver and Otter production and have purchased the rights to the aircraft, but in the meantime, Beavers can be found in better-than-new condition. They come out of specialist shops that custom rebuild them to factory-new standards with zero-time engines. They are better than new because they can incorporate any modifications of the customer's choice, and the rebuild provides attention to detail that is not possible on a factory assembly line.

In addition to the usual used Beaver market, a prime source for Beavers to rebuild are the military Beavers mothballed in various airplane bone yards worldwide.

The prime Beaver rebuilder is Kenmore Air Harbor in Seattle, Washington. The company was founded in 1946 and is one of the biggest floatplane operators in the world with a mixed fleet of 22 aircraft serving the Seattle and Vancouver areas. It is also the place to inquire about a better-than-new Beaver.

The rebuild process strips a Beaver down to its air-

Properly refurbished Beavers can fly forever.

frame skeleton. All parts are thoroughly cleaned for evaluation, magnafluxed for structural integrity, corroded components are discarded, and in most cases, the entire airframe is reskinned with new aluminum. The whole airframe also receives sophisticated anticorrosion treatment. Kenmore Air is the holder of the rights to EDO floats and can build a new set of floats for the airplane. The Wright engine is rebuilt to factory new tolerances and the desired airframe modifications are incorporated.

The most popular modifications include expanding the cabin space into the fuselage and adding two more windows, larger cargo doors, wingtip fuel tanks, a gross weight increase to 5,600 from 5,090 pounds, a Hartzell three-bladed propeller, and custom instrument panels. The extravagance of the interior and instrument panel is limited only by the customer's resources. A better-than-new Beaver doesn't come cheap. The most lavish rebuilds have gone for as much as five times their original factory-new price, but that doesn't seem to deter the demand. By 2003, Kenmore had rebuilt more than 140 of these peerless bushplanes, and quite a few of them were for private use.

Old-Fashioned Bush Flying

Bush flying in Canada continues to exist the old-fashioned way, mainly through companies like Air Dale, that serve wilderness tourism in its many forms. From Kenora, Ontario, Norsemen still haul passengers and freight into the bush. In the Northwest Territories, visitors to Great Bear Lake, Great Slave Lake, and others still come and go aboard a variety of aircraft on floats. They also transport fishing parties deep into the Barren Lands. On the Pacific Coast, a Grumman Goose or two go where wheeled planes cannot follow. There is a well-attended Norseman Reunion every year on Red Lake, Ontario.

Grumman Goose

Year introduced: 1937

Engine: 450-horsepower Pratt and Whitney Wasp (2)

Fuel: 200 gallons

Gross weight: 9,000 pounds

Payload (with full fuel): 1,700 pounds

Seats: 8

Cruise speed: 160 miles per hour

Highlights: It's a well-suited amphibian for the bush. It has plenty of power and good load bearing. The Goose was especially popular in southeast Alaska through the 1970s.

The Otter's double-slotted flaps are key to its excellent STOL performance. When fully extended, the inboard sections come down 60 degrees. The air flowing over the flap sections through the slots generates additional lift and reduces speed. Note that the ailerons are the lower segment of the outboard flap section. Taku Lodge is in the background.

Traditional bush-flying roles are now largely performed by modern commuter airlines and air taxis. The Canadian government's ambitious expansion of the aviation infrastructure, with its well-maintained hard-surface and gravel runways, into the country's remotest regions has taken hold. As the character of the business changed over the years, many of the old bush pilots changed with it. Among them was Ernie Boffa, who spent the final eight summers of his career working for Great Bear Lodge on Great Bear Lake in the Northwest Territories. He selected the fishing sites, set up camp, and flew and supported the fishing parties.

The client profile may have changed, but the job is still the same. As any young bush pilot soon finds out, wilderness tourists can be as trying as the most eccentric and cantankerous prospectors could be, like the fishing party Harvey Hobbs of Sault Ste. Marie had to fly to their lakeside camp when he worked in British Columbia. The four men and their gear for the five-day trip fit in the Beaver, but they also had to hire a Cessna 180 to carry their liquor supply. They were going to a camp without a radio and were told to raise a white flag in case of a serious problem. When Hobbs flew over them a few days later, the white flag was up. He landed with some apprehension only to find they were out of liquor.

A day before their scheduled return, the flag was flying again. This time they claimed they urgently needed a gun. When Hobbs asked who was after them, they said a bear was eating their fish. What they didn't say was that they were tossing their fish behind their cabin for four days instead of properly storing it as they had been instructed to do. Instead of a gun they received a lesson in storing fish and a tight-lipped pilot who took great pleasure in flying them out.

Another time another group had a legitimate bear problem. They had meticulously boxed their live fish and let the box down into the water at the end of a rope only to see a bear saunter up to the rope, reel in the box, flip it open, and eat the fish. And then there was . . .

And so the stories go. Fish stories, bear stories, and bush pilot tales. The reasons may be different, but the wilderness still beckons, just as it did when pilots like Noel Wien, Punch

Dickins, Bob Ellis, Frank Barr, Jim Dodson, Ernie Boffa, Don Braun, and so many others decided to make their life there and found it was a good one.

More travelers than ever take time off from their everyday lives and board jetliners and commuter aircraft to seek discretionary adventure in the wild places once sought by adventurers, mostly out to make a living. When they've gone as far into the wilderness as the airlines and commuters can fly them, there'll be a Super Cub on tundra tires or a Beaver on floats waiting to take them further into the wilderness.

The harsh, frigid beauty of the world of glaciers and lakes is a powerful draw for many bush pilots who prefer it to more conventional ways of making a living inside or outside the aviation industry.

A Piper Cub and a Bellanca Champion on Auk Lake in Alaska are parked by their owners as family cars are parked on the street elsewhere and are used the same way. The drooping wingtips on both aircraft are part of aftermarket STOL kits designed to enhance performance.

A turbine Otter arrives in Ketchikan on a dour, wet day. Combining the Otter and the Pratt & Whitney Canada PT6 turbine engine is a match made in heaven and gives the super STOL airframe the power it should have had originally, had it been available at the time.

The tilting dock is a clever way to easily lift this Cessna 185 out of the water for extended parking. The airplane is safer on a dry surface in high winds and waves.

When the fog rolls in, the floatplanes are a pretty sight their operator doesn't want to see. The lineup from front to back includes a Cessna 206, a Beaver, and a Turbine Otter. Bad weather wreaks havoc with the schedules of bushplanes restricted to flying in visual conditions. When the weather improves, clearing the passenger and cargo backlog can be a formidable task.

The water shimmers before the descending Beaver, like a lake of gold in a prospector's dream, as it reflects the late afternoon sun. The big radial engine's rattling roar fades to a muffled grumble as the power comes back. The floats touch so gently that the transition from air to water is imperceptible. At the right instant, the engine is shut down and the Beaver glides silently toward the shore. It loses all energy as it slides up the narrow, gravelly beach with a gentle crunch. Now there is total silence. Total isolation. The pilot has done what successful bush pilots have insisted is their only goal since the earliest days. The clients have been delivered from A to B. But the pilot is here for a lot more than that, and it is not the money. Soon the Beaver will leave and there will be no way out until it returns in a few days. For as long as there is a lake, a sandbar, or a strip of tundra where people want to go, far beyond the nearest airport or road, there will always be a bush pilot and a bushplane willing to take them there.

> *"Everybody used to think of pilots as being daring, flying in the north, but northern pilots were anything but daring. You were very, very careful."*
>
> —Max Ward

In spite of its hard-surface airport across the waterway, Ketchikan's waterfront looks much like it did when Ellis Air Transport's Grumman Goose fleet shuttled passengers between the docks and the airport on Annette Island 21 miles away.

A Beaver turns onto its final approach to the Lake Hood seaplane base. The big patch of water in the foreground is Lake Spenard, which was combined with Lake Hood (in the background) to create the water runway on the left side of lake and the taxiway to the right. Anchorage International Airport is to the left. A paved general aviation runway (not shown) is to the right. All three facilities are officially part of Anchorage International Airport and are run out of one tower.

Privately owned floatplanes are docked on Lake Hood, the world's busiest seaplane base.

When Lake Hood freezes over, it turns into the world's biggest ski plane base. Some of the best flying in Alaska is in the clear, calm, and short winter days.

Crossbow hunters wait for transportation during caribou season. Recreational business of all forms has mostly replaced other services provided by traditional bush flying in many areas.

On left, downwind to Bullchitna Lake for an exchange of fishing parties in the camps below. The Beaver will need a fraction of the lake surface to get in and out.

A successful hunt provides new problems for the hunter—how to safely transport the coveted trophy back to the family den in one piece on the airlines.

The Cessna 206 is as valued as the Beaver for smaller loads. Its higher speed, lower maintenance costs, and readily available parts are advantages it holds over the Beaver.

The Kahiltna Glacier in Denali National Park is 42 miles long and places the awesome scale of nature viewed from aloft in this part of the world into perspective.

There are hundreds of fishing camps in North America accessible by no other means except a floatplane.

A turbine Eurocopter operated by TEMSCO was the first large-scale helicopter operator in the Alaskan bush. Along with glacier tours, helicopters support logging, exploration, and scientific expeditions and have largely taken over rescue (not search) flights from fixed-wing aircraft.

A Turbine Otter is pictured low over the Ruth Glacier. Bush pilots need to develop excellent weather interpretation skills if they want to tangle with mountain valleys and passes. For the novice, it is tough to tell how long a pass will stay open in rapidly deteriorating weather. Mac McGee, owner of McGee Airways, liked to say, "I've got six airplanes, three of them in Rainy Pass."

Air Dale in Ontario, Canada, has been in the fishing, hunting, and adventure tourism business since the end of World War II with its own string of lodges served by its fleet of aircraft. Here an Air Dale Beaver is seen on Ranger Lake. It is a fairly stock aircraft with the original small round window and two-bladed propeller.

The Twin Otter was de Havilland Canada's next step beyond the Otter. It was an excellent STOL aircraft, but too expensive for many bush operators except for the larger ones. It found a popular niche as a commuter aircraft and set de Havilland Canada on course for the commuter business, which Bombardier continues today.

A Harbour Air Turbine Otter on floats serves the island communities off the coast of British Columbia, including Victoria, the province's capital.

A Beaver alights on tranquil waters. Its value is steadily going up as the Beaver is no longer made but remains one of the most desirable bushplanes.

Twin Otters on floats are also quite popular both for commuters and tourists. This Twin Otter flies a regular schedule in the Vancouver, British Columbia, area.

157

Bushplanes await the adventurous traveler when all other ways of getting there have been exhausted.

"Tourists are the biggest thing that Alaska can develop. We are counting on them as our long-range steady customers. We feel that people, more than goods, spell success for us."

—Ray Petersen

Bibliography

Borge, Jacques and Nicolas Viasnoff. *The Dakota*. New York: VILO, 1980.

Braun, Don C. with John C. Warren. *The Arctic Fox*. Back Bay Press, 1994.

Bruder, Gerry. *Heroes of the Horizon*. Portland, Oregon: Alaska Northwest Books, 1991.

Bruder, Gerry. *Northern Flights*. Boulder, Colorado: Pruett Publishing Co., 1988.

Bungey, Lloyd. *Pioneering Aviation in the West*. Surrey, British Columbia: Hancock House Publishers Ltd., 1992.

Bush Pilots, The. Alexandria, Virginia: Time-Life Books, Inc., 1983.

Cole, Dermot. *Frank Barr*. Portland, Oregon: Alaska Northwest Books, 1986.

Day, Beth. *Glacier Pilot*. New York: Henry Holt and Company, 1957.

Eichner, Ken. *Nine Lives of an Alaska Bush Pilot*. Bellingham, Washington: Taylor Press, 2002.

Ellis, Robert E. and Margaret R. Ellis. *What…No Landing Field?* Ketchikan, Alaska: The Bob Ellis Aviation Scholarship Foundation, 1998.

Foster, Tony. *The Bush Pilots*. San Jose, California: Authors Choice Press, 1990.

Gaede-Penner, Naomi, with Elmer E. Gaede. *Prescription for Adventure*. Castle Rock, Colorado: Change Points, 1991.

Grant, Robert. S. *Great Northern Bushplanes*. Surrey, British Columbia: Hancock House Publishers Ltd., 1997.

Greiner, James. *Wager With the Wind*. Chicago: Rand McNally & Company, 1978.

Harkey, Ira. *Pioneer Bush Pilot: The Story of Noel Wien*. University of Washington Press, 1974.

Jefford, Jack. *Winging It!* Anchorage: Alaska Northwest Books, 1981.

Keith, Ronald A. *Bush Pilot With a Briefcase*. Vancouver: Douglas & McIntyre, Ltd., 1972.

MacLean, Robert Merrill and Sean Rossiter. *Flying Cold*. Fairbanks, Alaska: Epicenter Press, 1994.

Mattson, Ted. *Adventures of the Iditarod Air Force*. Fairbanks, Alaska: Epicenter Press, Inc., 1997.

McAllister, Bruce and Corley-Smith, Peter. *Wings Over the Alaska Highway*. Boulder, Colorado: Roundup Press, 2001.

McAllister, Bruce. *Wings Above the Arctic*. Boulder, Colorado: Roundup Press, 2002.

McCaffrey, Dan. *Bush Planes and Bush Pilots*. Toronto: James Lorimer & Company, Ltd., 2002.

Mills, Stephen E. and James W. Phillips. *Sourdough Sky*. New York: Bonanza Books, 1960.

Murray, John and Nick Jans. Fodor's *Alaska*. Oakland, California: Compass American Guides, 2001.

Potter, Jean. *The Flying North*. New York: Curtis Publishing Co., 1945.

Rearden, Jim. *Arctic Bush Pilot*. Fairbanks, Alaska: Epicenter Press, Inc., 2000.

Rice, Robert. *An American Bush Pilot in Guyana*. Ann Arbor, Michigan: Proctor Publications, LLC, 2002.

Rossiter, Sean. *Otter & Twin Otter*. Vancouver: Douglas & McIntyre, 1998.

Rossiter, Sean. *The Immortal Beaver*. Vancouver: Douglas & McIntryre, 1996.

Ruotsala, Jim. *Alaskan Wings*. Juneau, Alaska: Seadrome Press, 2002.

Ruotsala, Jim. *Pilots of the Panhandle*. Juneau, Alaska: Seadrome Press, 1997.

Rychetnik, Joe. *Alaska's Sky Follies*. Fairbanks, Alaska: Epicenter Press, Inc. 1995.

Satterfield, Archie. *Alaska Bush Pilots in the Float Country*. Lincoln, Nebraska: Superior Publishing Co., 1969.

Satterfield, Archie. *The Alaska Airlines Story*. Anchorage, Alaska: Alaska Northwest Publishing Company, 1981.

Stedman, Bill. *The Bushed Pilot*. Petersburg, Alaska: Pilot Publishing, Inc., 1998.

Szurovy, Geza. *Classic American Airlines*. St. Paul, Minnesota: MBI Publishing Co., 2003.

Szurovy, Geza. *Private Pilot Magazine*, "House Calls Outback and Down Under." May 1989.

Theriault, George. *Trespassing in God's Country*. Chapleau, Ontario: Sunstar Publishing, Ltd., 1994.

Tordoff, Dirk. *Mercy Pilot*. Fairbanks, Alaska: Epicenter Press, 2002.

West, Bruce. *The Firebirds*. Ontario: J. C. Thatcher, 1974.

Whyard, Florence. *Ernie Boffa*. Anchorage, Alaska: Alaska Northwest Publishing Company, 1984.

Wixted, Edward P. *The North-West Aerial Frontier 1919-1934*. Brisbane, Queensland: Boolarong Publications, 1985.

Wood, Michael. *Go an Extra Mile*. London: William Collins Sons & Co., 1978.

Index